Promoting Yourself

Promoting Yourself

Yourself

50 Ways to Increase Your
Prestige, Power, and Paycheck

Marlene Caroselli, Ed.D.

SkillPath Publications
Mission, Kansas

Editor: Kelly Scanlon

Cover and Book Design: Rod Hankins

Library of Congress Catalog Card Number: 95-68998

ISBN: 1-878542-89-3

10   9   8   7   6   5   4   3   2   1   95   96   97   98   99

Printed in the United States of America

Contents

Preface

This book is a natural outgrowth of two recurring phenomena I encounter in the supervision/management/leadership classes I conduct:

1. Workers think their boss's job is easy and well-paying and wouldn't mind a shot at it themselves.

2. Managers and supervisors are reconsidering the pros and cons of their decision to go into management and wondering whether they may have erred in making that decision.

To be sure, I have encountered many excellent managers. They have the skills for directing and controlling the work lives of other people. They enjoy the challenge as well as the rewards of management. And, they are good at what they do.

There are numerous others, though, who were not sufficiently prepared for what the promotion would entail and who discover they really don't enjoy their new supervisory responsibilities. As author Wess Roberts asserts about management, "You gotta want to be in charge."

Management is not for everyone. *Promoting Yourself* was written to assure those who do not or cannot get the promotion they are seeking that there are numerous other ways to acquire the benefits that promotion would have given them.

It was also written as a reality check. "Be careful of what you wish for," the old saying goes, "for your wishes may come true." *Promoting Yourself* examines wishful thinking about management and offers appealing alternatives.

The management ranks are filled with those who have discovered too late that management really is not for them. Promotions inevitably mean changing your focus from your own achievements to orchestrating the achievements of others in order to reach a common goal. Perhaps you should be performing a solo concert instead of conducting others who may not even be reading from the same sheet of music.

No matter which path you have chosen to follow, you will find valuable information in this book—ideas for you to pursue when you can't be promoted or ideas for you to share with others who seek the rewards of promotion.

Introduction

In school, we worked hard to get good grades. And there were natural, positive consequences to that hard work: pleasing our parents, pleasing our teachers, pleasing ourselves, getting on the honor roll, getting into college, getting a scholarship, and so on. Many of us carry that hard-work syndrome into the workplace—believing that the most logical consequence of our conscientious performance will be a promotion.

And then reality hits: for every one promotional opportunity—according to Dr. Judith Bardwick in *The Plateau Trap*—there are 99 people who either want or are capable of holding that position. This Rule of 99 means that those who are not selected for the promotion will often blame themselves—when in truth the chances of being selected were very narrow indeed. There are numerous reasons to explain why we don't receive the promotions we seek. And most of those reasons have little to do with the hard work, loyalty, and commitment that ready-to-be-promoted employees have demonstrated over the years. In this era of downsizing, rightsizing, and corporate capsizing, the management ranks are narrowing, not expanding.

Beyond the limited opportunities for advancement, and despite the growing popularity of "horizontal" organizations, there is another reason would-be managers are reconsidering the decision to advance: Management simply "ain't all it's cracked up to be." Yes, there are rewards, but there are also these frustrations associated with supervision:

- Longer hours
- More responsibility
- Greater visibility and, therefore, greater scrutiny of one's work
- A loss of camaraderie with former peers
- Greater stress
- Less time to spend with family
- More human relations conflicts to deal with
- Additional learning
- Accountability for the actions of others
- More meetings
- A sense of isolation
- More bosses to report to/more "customers" to serve
- More administrative duties
- Weightier decisions to make
- Lack of support from various levels

And, as far as money is concerned, some managers realize that when they weigh the additional responsibilities and frustrations against the post-tax increase in salary, the promotion isn't as attractive as it once seemed. In fact, in many organizations, the operations managers earn less than those they supervise. That's because managers often work on a fixed salary, no matter how many hours they work. Other workers, however, are paid very well for the hours they work beyond the standard forty.

This book, then, discusses how to achieve satisfaction and self-growth in your job, even though promotion may not be a viable alternative. It offers positive steps you can take to increase your influence, importance, and income while contributing substantially to the mission of your organization. It will also help you explore ways to self-actualize, to enhance your individual and interpersonal effectiveness. (As an example, read the story of Helen Samett in the accompanying box.)

Consultant Peter Senge encourages employees to aspire to new heights and to imagine what can be different. That message is affirmed in these pages.

Finding a Cause...

**Helen Samett, Administrative Assistant to the President of
Lockheed Air Terminal, Inc.**

I moved to Los Angeles in 1977. While I had a very good position, it simply
was not enough for me, and I needed to find a purpose in life. I attended a
meeting with people in the entertainment industry who spoke about the deaths
of 45,000 children a day from malnutrition and preventable diseases. There I
learned the only thing keeping hunger in its terrible place was the lack of
political will of the people. The more I learned about the subject, the more
intense was my desire to do something about it.

I certainly was not alone. People like Jeff Bridges, Valerie Harper, Harvey
Korman, Gregory Peck and many others use their celebrity status to bring
awareness of this problem to the public. At that time, it was accepted that
hunger had to exist and children had to die. Also accepted was the feeling that
"I am just one person. How can I make a difference?" We knew we had to
change that.

For the last ten years, I have actively participated in RESULTS (Responsibility
for Ending Hunger Using Legislation, Trim-tabbing and Support). This is a
citizens' grassroots organization that strives to participate in our government, to
make changes in how our government spends money. We insist that money be
spent to help the millions of children, both in the United States and in
developing countries. The survival of children is our goal.

We meet in groups every month and learn about a piece of legislation that
could benefit the poor. We will study the bill, learn how to speak about it, and
write letters to our senators and representatives urging their support. We also
write letters to the editor that get published, along with our editorials and op-
ed pieces. We send copies of those to our legislators.

As a leader/spokesperson for the children who cannot speak for themselves, I
have developed a relationship with senators and representatives, meeting with
them in Washington, D.C., to seek their support on important issues. My most
memorable experience occurred when I was about to attend an international
conference in Washington. One of the things RESULTS does is write a bill and
then a senator and a representative present the bill before Congress. Our office

in Washington wrote a bill titled "The Global Poverty Reduction Act." We had two representatives who sponsored the bill in the House, but only one senator.

Prior to coming to Washington for the conference, I had the good fortune to meet Senator Tom Harkin. At that time, I was the executive assistant to a very prominent CEO in the housing industry. He had many contacts in Congress. However, every time any of them called him, they had to pass through me. I would always talk to them about RESULTS and enlist their support on our bills. When Senator Harkin came to our office, I quickly introduced myself to him and his aide. On his return to Washington, I called his office to set up an appointment.

Senator Harkin met with me and Sam Harris, the founder and executive director of RESULTS. Senator Harkin was chair of the Senate Appropriations Sub-committee. We told him about RESULTS and the bill we wanted him to co-sponsor. He saw the possibility of it becoming law and offered to introduce it in the Senate the very next morning. With his help, the bill, calling for measurable goals in areas such as infant mortality and literacy, went on to become part of our foreign aid policy.

I am proud to be part of an organization that has contributed so much to society. We have succeeded in making the end of hunger a world priority. We have seen the decline in the deaths of children—from 45,000 a day in 1979 to 35,000 a day in 1994. This is not good enough. There is much more to be done. I intend to continue lobbying, producing fund-raisers, writing letters, and speaking before groups to make a better world for all.

How This Book Is Organized

Promoting Yourself examines the three primary reasons people seek promotions—prestige, power, and paycheck—and offers you fifty alternatives for acquiring greater prestige, more power, or a bigger paycheck in spite of the diminishing likelihood of advancement or promotion.

These reasons form the book's three major sections. Within each section, you are asked to carefully examine the motivation behind your desire for a promotion and then consider the activities for satisfying those internal drives without having to climb the traditional ladder of success. Interspersed throughout the book are the personal commentaries of people who have found—outside their normal work activities—the personal satisfaction usually associated with career advancement.

The suggested activities, many of which include exercises to help you get started, are designed to appeal to all types of people, from the most conservative to those who get a thrill out of taking calculated risks. Some activities require more time and commitment than others. If a particular activity doesn't appeal to you or suit your personality or situation, read on until you find one that does. Turn to the book often for fresh ideas. There are enough suggestions in it to keep you busy for years. Most important, many of the activities are actually just a way of getting started. Most of them will lead you into other endeavors you may not have considered.

In the final section, "Biding Your Time," the employee who is still determined to seek advancement is given ideas for improving his or her chances of being chosen for the managerial ranks. For those of you who have decided to continue the climb up the corporate ladder, these suggestions will increase your visibility as you bide your time, waiting for the next opportunity to arise.

To begin, let's examine your personal reasons for seeking a promotion. Briefly answer each of the following questions:

- Why do you want a promotion? _____

  _____

- What do you think it will change? _____

  _____

- How will you work and interact differently with others? _____

  _____

- What positive changes will the promotion bring to your life? _____

  _____

- Who or what is influencing you to seek the promotion? _____

  _____

- What benefits will you realize? _____

  _____

- What advantages will a promotion provide that your current position cannot provide? _____

  _____

- As far as work is concerned, what arouses your passion and interest? _____

  _____

- Will a promotion include work on projects that interest you? _____

  _____

Study your answers. Do they point to a particular reason for wanting a promotion? Prestige, perhaps? Power, a desire to take charge and direct others? More money? If your answers point to one reason in particular, turn right to that section of the book and read the promotion alternatives suggested. If you're motivated by a combination of all three benefits, read through the entire book before choosing an activity.

Prestige

1

There's no doubt about it—there is a certain thrill in saying, "I have an important position." The words *supervisor* and *manager* carry connotations of success and responsibility. And there's nothing wrong with wanting a promotion because it will increase your prestige. Promotions are rewards for your dedication and achievement.

Those who feel their loyalty and productivity deserve recognition, though, often make the mistake of thinking that a promotion is the only way to achieve that recognition within the organizational structure. This is simply not the case.

The managerial ranks are thinning out. There is more security, many believe, in optimizing your "worker-bee" skills than in seeking the "queen-bee" position. Even though you may not be able to attain the lofty titles managers have (or used to have), you can attain the perquisites that accompany such titles. Greater prestige, power, and pay could be yours with fewer headaches and less stress than most managers have.

Before you take the quiz on the next page, explore your intention to acquire greater prestige by filling out this self-assessment.

1. These are five words I associate with prestige:

_____   _____

_____   _____

_____

2. Of the eight terms in this "prestige circle," which is most important to you?

3. Which term did you select? _____
   Explain its importance to you. _____

   _____

4. Is there another term that defines an aspect of prestige that is important to you? If so, write it here: _____

Explain its importance: _____

_____

5. Regarding the term(s) you chose as being an important part of prestige, explain how greater prestige would alter you (your attitude, your behavior, your capability) in terms of the work you do.

_____

_____

_____

6. Many people seek greater prestige not so much for themselves but rather as a derivative benefit to those with whom they share their lives. Who would be pleased by the greater prestige that might accrue to you?

_____ _____

_____ _____

_____ _____

7. Whose increased prestige makes you proud(er)?

_____ _____

_____ _____

_____ _____

8. Disregarding high salaries, who in your organization has prestige?

_____

_____

Based on what factors? _____

_____

9. Whose prestige path would you like to follow? _____

Directions: For each of the following statments, check "T" for true or "F" for false.

T   F

☐ ☐ 1. I do not believe in "hiding my light under a bushel."

☐ ☐ 2. I am pleased when my work is recognized because I do strive for excellence.

☐ ☐ 3. I am somewhat of a perfectionist.

☐ ☐ 4. It is important that my family be proud of my achievements.

☐ ☐ 5. I believe in working for more than a paycheck.

☐ ☐ 6. I have been achievement-oriented since I was in high school.

☐ ☐ 7. I do not believe in false modesty.

☐ ☐ 8. Receiving feedback on my work is important.

☐ ☐ 9. I have had people other than my boss compliment me on my work.

☐ ☐ 10. It is important to me to be satisfied with my work.

If you answered "true" to the majority of these questions, you are probably the sort of person who is not ashamed of your excellence and enjoy the recognition associated with it. You believe in working hard for what you believe is important in life. And one of the things you believe is important is doing well in your career. The seventeen recommendations that follow are ways you can achieve recognition and prestige without being promoted.

# PROMOTION ACTIVITY #1:

Become an officer in an organization.

Make your own good fortune. If you really enjoy the prestige that comes with outstanding work but find that your outstanding work will not lead to a promotion any time soon, then look around you.

There are opportunities everywhere to make a name for yourself, to utilize the overflowing talents you possess. In fact, you may have energy, skills, and ambition that outweigh your job requirements. Use these to tackle some new projects.

One possibility is to tap into your natural leadership and seek an officer's position in an association—either one in the workplace or one in a professional organization related to your line of work.

There is another possibility, of course. You could form your own organization. That's what a group of secretaries did at Mount Carmel Medical Center in Columbus, Ohio. They've been holding regular but informal meetings for the last several years. Named ASSET (Administrative Support/Secretarial Enrichment Team), the group plans and conducts educational training for the support staff at the hospital. They have made such a name for themselves that often—at executive-level meetings— someone will suggest, "Why don't we run this idea by ASSET and see what they have to say?"

Consider also the creative solution of Joan "JJ" MacHill, a service representative for a salaried savings plan at a major aerospace firm (see box).

Add some creativity to your organizational skills and you should soon be able to find a prestige-opportunity opening up for you. Just imagine your name and new title at the bottom of your correspondence or on your business card! There's a whole world of inviting possibilities out there.

Officer Opportunities...

Joan "JJ" MacHill, Service Representative, Aerospace Firm

All of my working life, I have played a supporting role. And I do not mind having locked myself into this situation. As a matter of fact, I prefer it. I would not want the headaches associated with my boss's job. And yet, I have found that I am seeking something beyond an auxiliary position.

Fortunately, I have found a certain degree of prestige in the position I hold in our corporate management association. There I serve as the vice president of programs, and that is how I sign my name when I am conducting business for our association.

Serving as vice president of programs has opened a lot of doors for me. It has allowed me to do things and meet people that simply are not part of the purview of my regular job.

I have some cheerleader tendencies, I must admit, and there really are not many cheerleading needs in my work as a service representative. But our management association is a different story. There, I can allow my enthusiasm to spill over as we plan to bring some really distinguished speakers in to address our managers.

PROMOTION ACTIVITY #2:

Present a proposal to your boss.

One excellent way to acquire more prestige than you currently enjoy is to propose an idea to your boss. You don't have to go far out on a limb—especially not the first time. But get in the habit of routinely proposing a new idea or a new purchase or an improvement in the work process. Demonstrate your initiative by doing some research on your own—without being asked to.

Do your homework and then either meet with your boss or send a memo outlining your proposal. In the best of all possible business worlds, your boss will credit you with the new idea. Newfound prestige will be yours via the complimentary words of others whom your boss tells about your accomplishments.

The following exercise provides some prompts to start you thinking about worthwhile recommendations you might make to your boss.

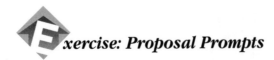

Exercise: Proposal Prompts

1. What are some ways that time, money, or resources are being wasted in our department or organization?

_____

_____

_____

2. How are other offices or organizations handling similar processes?

_____

_____

3. How can we inexpensively improve or increase employee training?

_____

_____

4. Which publications should we be subscribing to that we aren't?

_____

_____

5. What could we do to improve our orientation program?

_____

_____

6. How can we improve our reward/recognition system?

_____

_____

7. What can we do to improve wellness?

_____

_____

8. How could we celebrate National Quality Month in October?

_____

_____

9. In what ways could we increase our knowledge of the various cultures represented in our workplace?

_____

_____

# PROMOTION ACTIVITY #3:

Begin a tradition.

There was a time in America when there was no Mother's Day or Martin Luther King Day. There was a time when Earth Day did not exist and a period before April was declared Secretaries Month. Although you certainly do not need to set such grandiose goals, do think about a local event you can plan. When you do, make certain to get media coverage. Peter Jennings may not find your event sufficiently important for the evening news, but you should be able to get the company newsletter to give you a few inches of space.

Although your tradition may start out small, it will catch on if it is a good idea and if it captures the interest of your co-workers.

Try the tradition-starting strategy that begins on page 20. As you work through each step, be sure to keep a notebook of possible traditions you could start. Consider, for example, the case of Marilyn Lewis, who began a tradition of her own (see box). Although acquiring personal power was not her primary goal, she found, as you will, that her visibility increased as she undertook new projects. By seeking to help others, she indirectly helped herself.

Cocoon-Busting Exemplar...

Marilyn Lewis, Executive Secretary, Los Angeles County Coroner's Office, Los Angeles, California

"I've always been a little odd," Marilyn Lewis confesses. It's the oddness that has resulted in more than one cocoon-busting endeavor. In this case, it's an idea for raising money that has brought this 21-year-veteran of the Coroner's Office worldwide fame.

Her idea: put a "Sherlock" logo on a number of products and sell them around the world. (The proceeds go to a juvenile drunk-driving program in Los Angeles.) The program—which now includes 23 items, such as a body outline on a beach towel—has grossed over $300,000. Its success has led Marilyn Lewis to a new job and a new title: she is now the marketing coordinator for the Los Angeles County Coroner's Office. With pride, this chance-taking nonconformist regards her program as the "Nordstroms" of the Coroner's Office.

"We're here to serve," this self-proclaimed perpetual youngster declares.

"I don't worry about getting into trouble with my ideas," Marilyn admits. "When I feel strongly about something, I will take a stand. I don't always know why I'm getting involved and I don't always know why I do things but I have a strong sense of what has to be done. I don't mind giving something extra but I do mind being 'clocked in and clocked out.'"

You need a daring spirit, Marilyn asserts. You need to become involved. She admits she likes to go beyond the rules. While she respects policies and procedures, she knows they can sometimes trap a good idea, restrain a far-reaching vision, ensnare creativity in a spider's web of protocol. She simply brushes cobwebs aside in order to transform her ideas into organizational realities.

A willingness to shift paradigms, to circumvent obstacles, characterizes the Emerging Woman. Marilyn exemplifies this "can-do" spirit as she traces the steps behind her innovative idea. The unofficial "Sherlock" logo was intended to be upbeat—more in the nature of an intriguing whodunit than a virtual reality image. The thousands of letters she has received affirm her faith that a little marketing can go a long way to raise monies for a good cause.

With a few strategic calls from Marilyn, the local press and media became interested in the story. So did readers of the AP wire stories. Marilyn wound up being featured on the evening news with Tom Brokaw. The story also ran in *Newsweek* and the *Wall Street Journal,* and Marilyn has had calls from people in Australia, the Netherlands, Norway, and England.

Her advice for others seeking to develop the cocoon-busting spirit:
- Regard turning negatives into positives as a personal challenge.
- Do things without being asked.
- Take chances.
- Have faith in your own capabilities.
- Believe there can be a better way.
- Do not be discouraged by initial rejection.
- Build on past experiences.

"Some places discourage free thinking," she acknowledges. "Most people like to keep things the way they are. But I am right-brained—I like to have a vision, to figure out how I can improve processes. I have faith that things can get better and I nudge them along a bit by learning all I can."*

* Excerpted with permission from *Cocoon-busters: Stories of Emerging Women,* Dr. Marlene Caroselli, published by the Center for Professional Development, 1995.

Exercise: Tradition-Starting Strategy

1. Keep abreast of local and national happenings. Read the daily newspaper to discover what others are doing. Be receptive to new knowledge and allow it to spark ideas. Keep a notebook of possible traditions to start.

2. Check around. What other "traditions" already exist? You probably have an annual company picnic. Or a recycling program. Or an awards banquet. Or a company library. Talk to the people who have initiated those events and programs. Ask about obstacles they had to overcome as they started them.

3. Make a few phone calls outside the company. Learn what others have done and how they did it. In most cases, you will find professional colleagues more than willing to share. Be certain, of course, to acknowledge their help with a letter of appreciation.

4. Make a list of all those you'll need approval from before undertaking your project. Ask your boss to "approve" the list before you contact the individuals.

5. Decide who could assist you in this undertaking. Who has special talents or excellent connections? Who is unafraid of hard work? Whom can you trust to follow through on agreed-upon plans?

6. Don't overlook the cost factor. Although many of the best traditions began with very little capital, you will want to guarantee the success of your idea by having enough money to launch the project. Confer with others to learn how you can acquire or raise that money.

7. Prepare a schedule of milestone events and the dates by which you hope to achieve them.

8. Don't overlook the power of "strategic alliances." With what other groups or individuals—inside or outside your organization—could you form a partnership in order to implement this project?

9. Line up as many participants as you can to be involved with the unveiling of your plan or the scheduling of the first annual event. Success tends to be self-perpetuating, but you must do all you can to ensure positive results with a first-time change in the way you conduct business or pleasure.

10. Give as much advance publicity as you can to the change you are proposing. Then—after you have held several dry runs or pilot programs to test your plan—launch your project. And smile graciously as the praise and prestige follow.

PROMOTION ACTIVITY #4:

Work to establish "flow" in the office.

Write down your most satisfying experience: _____

_____

_____

_____

_____

This is the request Mihaly Csikszentmihalyi of the University of Chicago made of hundreds of people. Csikszentmihalyi has spent nearly thirty years of his life trying to determine what makes people happy. Not surprisingly, when people detailed their happiest memories, those moments were usually associated with meeting a challenge, with facing a difficult situation head on, and emerging victorious.

In his highly acclaimed book *Flow: The Psychology of Optimal Experience,* Csikszentmihalyi shares a synthesis of people's responses to his request. He uses the word *flow* to describe those moments—some of them painful—that we struggle through to overcome hardships or deadlines. Psychologists find "flow" in those moments that may stretch us to our physical or mental limits, but later leave us feeling elated by the success we have achieved.

Writing in *Success* magazine, Duncan Maxwell Anderson and Richard Poe describe "flow" as "a state of total absorption in work, coupled with pride in achievement." Anderson and Poe note that when people are in the flow stage, they are able to surpass their usual standards in terms of the quality and quantity of the work they produce (June 1992, p. 32).

Make it a priority to help others achieve that intense state of complete satisfaction with, and total absorption in, the work they are doing. The sharing and esprit de corps that result when people are working cooperatively—not competitively—may already exist in your office. If so, attempt to be a *flow-sustainer.*

In all likelihood, though, your colleagues are so caught up in their individual responsibilities that the collective excitement of seeing a difficult project through to successful completion does not occur often. In this case, try the following exercise to establish "flow."

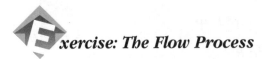

Exercise: The Flow Process

To establish "flow," follow these steps:

1. Buy a copy of *Flow*. Read it, underlining passages that are particularly relevant for certain colleagues. Prepare an easy-to-read synopsis of the book or of your favorite excerpts.

2. Loan your book, one at time, to the individuals you identified in Step #1 who would really understand or respond to the underlined passages you have identified for them.

3. As you wait for the book to be returned to you, entice others with short examples from the book. Build up some excitement, but don't overdo it.

4. Start a list of the barriers people cite, the reasons they give for why it might be hard to achieve a state of "flow." Then prepare to explain how those barriers could be eliminated—at least as many of them as possible.

5. Once you have these converts, share your synopsis with everyone in the office. Explain that you were really impressed by the book and that you think it would be worthwhile if the office could replicate the "flow" atmosphere, if only for a specified period.

6. For that specified period, put aside your usual persona and become a cheerleader, coach, obstacle-remover, booster, minister, and anything else necessary to optimize the efforts of your colleagues. You may be able to reach the "flow" state only once a year, but during that time, people will feel better about themselves than they usually do. And the gratitude will "flow" to you for having reminded your co-workers of the joy to be found in a job done well.

PROMOTION ACTIVITY #5:

Form a team.

Although promotions may not be plentiful, the current business environment *does* offer multiple opportunities for people who have an important leadership contribution to make. Serving as a team leader is an excellent way to acquire the kind of prestige managers have without assuming the responsibilities they are held accountable for.

More and more organizations are moving toward the team concept. In fact, a survey by *Training* magazine found that 82 percent of all American firms have some employees working in groups identified as teams. If you haven't yet served on a team, make it a point to join one or form one before the year is over. Once you have some team experience under your belt, you can serve as team leader.

The benefits of teamwork are numerous for both the individual and the organization:

- Increased employee empowerment
- Better quality of goods and services
- Greater morale
- Greater profits
- More satisfied customers
- Increased productivity

Even if you are self-employed, you can consider forming a looser type of team or network involving your suppliers and your customers. And don't forget how valuable teams can be in carrying out volunteer projects.

Use the Team Formation Guide on the next page to determine the kind of project and the kind of team you could form.

Exercise: Team Formation Guide

A. What Will the Team Do?

1. What is a valuable project we could undertake? _____

_____

_____

or 2. What is a process that we could improve (in terms of time, errors, cost, or steps)?

_____

_____

or 3. What is a problem that needs to be solved? _____

_____

_____

B. Who Will Serve on the Team?

Six to eight members is the ideal size. Consider:

1. Who is very creative? _____

2. Who is very practical? _____

3. Who is very knowledgeable? _____

4. Who cares about this a great deal? _____

5. Who has special talents we could use? _____

6. Who has facilitation skills? _____

C. Additional Considerations

1. Where, when, how long, and how often could we meet? _____

_____

_____

2. Would our team's goal support the organizational mission?

_____

_____

3. What resources would we need?

_____

_____

_____

_____

4. Whose approval do we need before we undertake this team effort?

_____

_____

_____

5. What is the time frame for accomplishing our goal?

_____

_____

_____

6. What are some possible pitfalls we should be considering?

_____

_____

_____

7. What kinds of data do we need to collect?

_____

_____

_____

8. Who could be our "champion"?_____

_____

9. Where could we obtain information or precedents so we don't have to reinvent the wheel at each stage of completion?

_____

_____

_____

Being a team leader is not an easy task, but each time you serve as one, your professional excellence and, therefore, prestige will grow. Even teams that do not succeed in their original intentions nonetheless succeed in having learned some valuable lessons about team dynamics, establishing and reaching goals, solving problems, and collecting data.

Few things feel as good as the pride that successful teams experience. The prestige associated with team accomplishments is a collective pride rather than an individual one, but it is an undeniable source of satisfaction for all concerned.

PROMOTION ACTIVITY #6:

Initiate a culture-enhancing project.

Consider what office life was like in the 1800s. The following set of office rules was found in the files of a firm moving to a new location in Boston. It was originally published in the *Boston Sunday Herald* of October 5, 1858.

1. Office employees each day will fill lamps, clean chimneys, and trim wicks. Wash windows once a week.

2. Each clerk will bring in a bucket of water and a scuttle of coal for the day's business.

3. Make your pens carefully. You may whittle nibs to your individual taste.

4. Men employees will be given an evening off each week for courting purposes, or two evenings a week if they go regularly to church.

5. After thirteen hours of labor in the office, the employee should spend the remaining time reading the Bible and other good books.

6. Every employee should lay aside from each pay day a goodly sum of his earnings for his benefit during his declining years so that he will not become a burden to society.

7. Any employee who smokes Spanish cigars, uses liquor in any form, or frequents pool and public halls or gets shaved in a barber shop, will give good reason to suspect his worth, intentions, integrity, and honesty.

8. The employee who has performed his labor faithfully and without fault for five years will be given an increase of five cents per day in his pay providing profits from business permit it.

Think now about the unofficial (and probably unrecorded) rules of conduct that govern your office. Write an Employees' Bill of Rights—in either a serious or facetious tone. Get permission to publicly post it or transmit it by e-mail. Then focus on one of the workplace expectations you listed and see what you can do to improve it. For example, if you write "Every employee deserves to be listened to," you might think of ways to improve the listening skills of your colleagues. You could circulate articles about listening or invite a guest lecturer to address a lunchtime audience or convince the training department to hold a class on listening skills. Or, you could work to improve the suggestion system so that employees' ideas have a better chance of being heard or considered.

Further, if you list as a "right" the fact that every employee deserves recognition for his or her ideas, you could compile a list of ways to recognize employees without spending exorbitant amounts of money. Give the list to your boss and ask him or her to share it with other managers.

Remember that prestige seldom flows to invisible people. With a project such as this, you will increase not only your own prestige but also your colleagues' feelings of self-worth.

PROMOTION ACTIVITY #7:

Find promotion alternatives.

Consider what Owen Edwards has to say about the upward spiral of careers ("Seven Deadly Sins of Management," *Working Woman,* March 1992, p. 82):

> Luckily, blind ambition is no longer the only survival mode. In response to flattened hierarchies (fewer management jobs) and in order to reduce the kind of one-against-all competitiveness that for years has raised hell (and lowered productivity), companies like GE, Monsanto and Pacific Gas & Electric have introduced programs to encourage executives to stay in their jobs longer or to move laterally and like it. Monsanto has created over 100 fellowships for scientists not interested in corporate positions. The idea is to offer rewards like higher pay and more responsibility for effective work rather than a constant upward movement.

What is your company doing to dampen promotion desires without dampening enthusiasm? What are other companies doing? Make a few phone calls. Read a few articles. Begin to compile a list of alternatives. Decide which of the programs—in full or in part—would work in your organization.

Then, when you have formulated a plan that you think will work—for you and possibly for others as well—present it to your boss. You have a cause. Now become a champion. Your Promotion Alternative Plan could easily become a win-win situation for all involved.

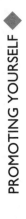

Exercise: Promotion Alternative Plan

Do some research into what other organizations are offering as alternatives to promotions. Would any of them work in your organization? Conduct some unofficial surveys of your co-workers to find out what types of recognition are appealing when promotions aren't an option. Write your results on this page and organize it into a Promotion Alternative Plan you could present to your supervisor.

# PROMOTON ACTIVITY #8:

Form a strategic alliance.

Look around you. Everywhere you turn are dozens of examples of alliances—partnerships between groups that in the past had little or no connection with one another. The synergy that results from these alliances enriches both groups. What alliances could you form with other companies? Other countries? No matter what level of the organization you work at, forming a strategic alliance is not as hard as you may think.

For example, a professional trainer and consultant was asked to conduct some workshops in Singapore. Following her return to the United States, her associate in Singapore asked whether they could become transoceanic partners. He asked if he could describe her firm as his American subsidiary and offered her a description of his firm as *her* subsidiary. Albeit an informal alliance, his vision has helped pave the way for more international work for her and more American connections for him.

Or consider Nancy Shairer, who is a senior executive secretary at Bausch and Lomb, headquartered in Rochester, New York. She has been instrumental in forming a Secretaries Council and in promoting educational opportunities for secretaries at the giant optical care company. (Eleven percent of the secretaries at Bausch and Lomb hold the CPS [Certified Professional Secretary] rating.)

In terms of "local" strategic alliances, Shairer has found supporters within the management ranks of Bausch and Lomb for the endeavors she and her committee are pursuing. In terms of more "global" alliances, Shairer disseminates, to secretarial teams throughout the country, information on how to start and maintain a successful team within the organizational structure. She is also process leader of the Rochester Intercompany Secretarial Roundtable, a group of fifty secretaries from sixteen local companies who meet twice a year to discuss topics of mutual interest.

The average person has average experiences. But if you are willing to think beyond your existing confines, you will find above-average experiences and prestige awaiting you.

Exercise: Forming Strategic Alliances Worksheet

Think of some strategic alliances you can form with others inside or outside your company, your professional field, your state or nation. The first step in forming this all-important connection is just a phone call or a letter away.

Alliance _____

    Benefits for You _____

    Benefits for Partner_____

Alliance _____

    Benefits for You _____

    Benefits for Partner_____

Alliance _____

    Benefits for You _____

    Benefits for Partner_____

Alliance _____

    Benefits for You _____

    Benefits for Partner_____

Alliance _____

    Benefits for You _____

    Benefits for Partner_____

Alliance _____

    Benefits for You _____

    Benefits for Partner_____

Alliance _____

    Benefits for You _____

    Benefits for Partner_____

# PROMOTION ACTIVITY #9:

Conduct a seminar.

Stan Bartosiak, a middle school history teacher in Glendale, California, loves what he does: teaching kids. He is satisfied with his lot in life and feels fortunate that he is able to fulfill his life's ambition. There are times, however, when he longs for a bit of acclaim beyond what his students give him.

So, Bartosiak represents the union for the California Teachers Association, a contingent of the National Education Association. As a representative, he has traveled to conferences in various parts of the country. In addition to his teaching responsibilities, he conducts seminars on weekends for large companies in Southern California. His topics include "Thinking on Your Feet (Without Putting Them in Your Mouth)," "Effective Listening," "Writing for Work," and "Perfect Proofreading."

The average teacher would consider this to be a full enough academic plate. But not Bartosiak. As a mentor teacher, he also conducts seminars for fellow teachers— on topics such as SDAIE (Specifically Designed Academic Instruction in English)— making content curriculum accessible to students of limited English ability, cooperative learning, conflict resolution, and cultural diversity.

As he acquires stature on a larger and larger scale, Bartosiak acknowledges that the opportunities he has created for himself have led to other opportunities, to new experiences, to new people, and to new sources of income.

Do you have something to offer others? Of course you do. We all do. Would you like to create a niche for yourself and possibly earn some additional money as well? On the next page is a seminar survey designed to help you consider your possibilities for developing and presenting a seminar. Answer the questions and then take some action.

Exercise: Seminar Survey

1. What subjects do you know a lot about? _____

_____

_____

2. Which of these subjects would be interesting to the people who live in your community or with whom you work? _____

_____

_____

3. Which subject would lend itself to a one-hour presentation?

_____

_____

4. How would you organize that presentation? _____

_____

_____

_____

_____

_____

_____

_____

5. What points of interest, anecdotes, statistics, and examples could you add to lend vitality to your presentation? _____

_____

_____

_____

_____

_____

6. What steps would you have to take, whose approval would you need to obtain, what arrangements would you have to make if you were to offer this presentation as a lunch-time lecture at work? _____

_____

_____

_____

_____

7. If you were to present this seminar in your community, what groups would be interested? _____

_____

_____

Additional Seminar Survey Notes

_____

_____

_____

_____

_____

_____

_____

_____

_____

_____

_____

_____

_____

_____

_____

Now, based on the information you gathered in your survey, prepare a proposal outlining what your presentation would look like, what the benefits would be to the participants, your background, and what fee (if any) you would charge. Submit the proposal to the appropriate individuals.

Follow up to learn of their decision. If your proposal is rejected, try to learn why so you can avoid those roadblocks in the next proposal you prepare. Expand your thinking until you find an audience that will profit from your knowledge. Think of volunteer groups in your community. Contact the library, local seminar presenters, and national training firms. Keep working until success is yours.

# PROMOTION ACTIVITY #10:

Become a "piece of pepperoni" in the organizational pie.

James A. Thompson, writing in *Organizations In Action,* discusses how organizational changes make new opportunities and new coalitions possible. Organizations in the "reinvention" mode are indeed finding that the very foundations of organizations are shifting.

Like the walls of Jericho and East Germany, the walls of many corporations are figuratively tumbling down. At Eastman Chemical Company, for example, the familiar organizational chart no longer exists. In its place is a "pizza chart," so-called because it looks like a pizza covered with pepperoni. Explains Ernest Deavenport, Jr., the company's president, "We did it in circular form to show that everyone is equal in the organization. No one dominates the others. The white space inside the circle is more important than the lines" (*Business Week,* ibid., p. 80).

Stake out a claim to your own white space. Define your piece of pepperoni. For example, in the break room of a federal agency in Flagstaff, Arizona, a sign on the wall proudly proclaims:

> "This is *our* break room. Help me make it a place we enjoy coming to. Keep it clean. Keep it quiet. Keep it going by contributing to our fund."

The notice is signed "The Coffee Czarina." Everyone there knows exactly who she is. She has assumed authority over the operation of the room and its accoutrements. She has designated her own sphere within the larger organization.

You may wish your sphere to be more professional than lighthearted. No matter what kind of contribution you wish to make to the organizational pie, the worksheet on the next page will help you make it an appropriate one.

Exercise: Carving Out Your Piece of the Pie

In today's circular organization, there are multiple partnerships—arrangements and agreements and cooperative relationships among the numerous centers of excellence. If you were to establish your own center, your own pepperoni piece on the organizational pizza, what would that center be? Whether you make your center a formal or an informal one, whether it is officially sanctioned or unofficially operated, it should represent a contribution you are willing to make above and beyond what your official job requires.

This chart should help.

In the "Skill" column, place a circle beside any position you could unofficially hold within the office or within the organization. Then look at all the positions with circles and select one that would yield the most prestige in the eyes of your boss or other influential individuals. Place a star beside that one position. Then use the lines in the final column to define how your skills could be utilized by your employer.

Position	Skill	Prestige	Ways I Could Contribute
Accountant			_____
Activity planner			_____
Administrative assistant			_____
Advertising executive			_____
Arbitrator			_____
Artist			_____
Auditor			_____
Banker			_____
Booking agent			_____
Buyer			_____
Communications consultant			_____
Community liaison			_____
Coordinator			_____

Position	Skill	Prestige	Ways I Could Contribute
Copywriter			_____
Counselor			_____
Design engineer			_____
Editor			_____
Fund-raiser			_____
Journalist			_____
Librarian			_____
Lobbyist			_____
Management consultant			_____
Manager			_____
Market analyst			_____
Photographer			_____
Public relations officer			_____
Rehabilitative physiotherapist			_____
Researcher			_____
Sales			_____
Social worker			_____
Sociologist			_____
Systems analyst			_____
Teacher			_____
Travel agent			_____
Writer			_____

PROMOTION ACTIVITY #11:

Do volunteer work.

Psychologists have long documented the need to find meaning in our lives. For most of us, work provides one source of significance. Through our jobs, we validate the contribution we can make; we find opportunities to make a difference, to help, to give back.

Of course, there are other sources that offer the prestige associated with doing important work. The volunteer organization is one. Apart from the good feelings altruism always generates, you will meet interesting people, have a chance to make decisions about events outside your workday, and soon acquire pride in accomplishment.

Begin by deciding where you would like to channel your energies. Then contact your local newspaper, library, or phone book to learn which volunteer agencies support the cause you are interested in.

Assume, for example, that you are concerned about refugee children in various parts of the world. The list of volunteer agencies for this one cause alone should give you more than enough to do with any spare time you may have.

If there is no established group for the cause you are interested in, consider starting one.

PROMOTION ACTIVITY #12:

Become an honorary consul.

Many countries establish consulates in large cities. These honorary consulates assist with the official work being done by the country's formally recognized embassy in Washington, D.C. It's possible to become a diplomat for one of these consulates if there is one in your city.

If world politics and geography have long interested you, this may be just what you've been looking for. The honorary consul is expected to assist Americans who wish to travel to or conduct business with other countries. You'd also be expected to provide information about visas, exports, and so forth.

To start? Contact the Washington embassy of the country you'd like to represent. (Selecting a company that your company does business with would be a wise move.) Representatives will advise you of what you need to do to proceed with your plans.

PROMOTION ACTIVITY #13:

Step out of your comfort zone.

Raquel Jackson, a computer assistant at the Naval Surface Warfare Center, Port Hueneme Division, Fleet Combat Direction Systems Support Activity at Dam Neck in Virginia Beach, is the perfect example of a self-promoter. In addition to her work, she is a charter member of the area Toastmasters Club, serving as president for two years and as area governor for the past year. She stepped out of her comfort zone and into the spotlight of prestige in the following way.

While attending a conference in Kansas City, she offered an opinion during the question-and-answer period. Her thoughts were so lucid that the audience applauded. One member of the audience approached her and asked whether she had ever considered giving workshops. Her first thought was, "This is a new pickup line." Nonetheless, they discussed the possibility, exchanged cards, and went their separate ways. She never heard from him again.

However, a year later, she received a call from someone the stranger had given her name to. The caller asked whether Raquel would come to Washington, D.C., to give a workshop. She did and was asked back four times. She has also conducted Equal Employment Opportunity (EEO)-sponsored workshops at the naval base. By stepping out of her comfort zone and pursuing these speaking opportunities, Raquel was able form her own company.

Speaking skills are vital for career success. Almost everyone feels comfortable speaking one-on-one, but many people are uncomfortable in front of groups. Just remember that as you learn to speak in front of larger and larger audiences, your self-confidence will grow.

You, too, should expand the size of your comfort zone. Doing so increases your opportunities for growth. Use the chart on the next page to assist you. Think of five entries, if possible, for each of the concentric circles that symbolize the aspects of your life. Think long and hard about ways to minimize the final circle ("Paralyzes me with fear; would rather die than attempt it") and ways to maximize the center circle ("Makes me feel very comfortable; as easy as sinking my thumb into chocolate frosting").

Exercise: Comfort and Discomfort Zones

What five things do you feel very comfortable doing?

_____

_____

_____

_____

_____

What five things are you learning to do well and comfortably?

_____

_____

_____

_____

_____

What five things are you resisting but need to learn to do well?

_____

_____

_____

_____

_____

What five things are you extremely uncomfortable doing?

_____

_____

_____

_____

_____

Now look over all the entries in all the categories. Select five that hold the most promise for increasing your prestige. Don't overlook the opportunities you may be passing up because you'd feel uncomfortable pursuing one or more of the activities. Then prioritize your list from 1 to 5, with 1 being the item that is most likely to increase your prestige.

Rank   Item

_____   _____

_____   _____

_____   _____

_____   _____

_____   _____

Finally, describe how you can convert that prestige potential into reality. What steps will you take ?

_____

_____

_____

_____

_____

_____

_____

_____

_____

_____

_____

_____

_____

_____

PROMOTION ACTIVITY #14:

Build a better trench.

In *Managing With a Heart,* author Sharon Good observes that the people "in the trenches" often understand the operation better than the "generals" do. Even though you are in the metaphoric trench, take time to look above and over the dirt to see what other trenches look like. Do not assume you have the perfect trench or that problems cannot arise within your trench.

Consider a problem (or a future problem) you are experiencing with some aspect of your job. Think about it, talk to co-workers about it, get books from the library about it, find out what other companies are doing about it. Promise yourself that within two months, you will have found a way to solve this problem or, at the very least, to lessen the negative impact it is having on you, your co-workers, or the work process.

Go beyond the proposal and concept stage to create a solution to the problem. It may be a new form, a new filing system, a new way to conduct meetings, a new team to assist patients' families in the emergency room. Who knows what amorphous entity awaits your creativity? Transform it from a vague promise into a workable and profitable way of doing business. Then test it to find out whether it works better than the existing procedure.

Begin by asking others (both inside and outside your organization) for their input. You may wish to use the "A-D-D" form on the next page. Once you have obtained their feedback, including your boss's, take steps to make it part of the routine.

Your job does not end with the creation stage, however. Once you have implemented your concept, you must work to continuously evaluate its effectiveness and make adjustments when and where needed.

Exercise: A - D - D Approach to Making Good Ideas Better

State here what you are planning to create, what your output will be:

_____

_____

_____

_____

_____

_____

_____

_____

_____

_____

A = Amplify: Get input from others about the idea. Specifically, ask how they would amplify or add to the idea you are proposing. What is missing from the idea you have described? What have you overlooked? What are others doing that might be incorporated into this plan? What has been omitted? (Encourage them to focus only on this aspect now. They'll have an opportunity to offer their ideas on other aspects later.)

_____

_____

_____

_____

_____

_____

_____

_____

_____

D = Deduct: Ask your reviewers what, specifically, they would subtract from the concept you are proposing. Where is it too broad? Where does it overreach appropriate boundaries? Where is it too ambitious? What parts may not be relevant?

_____

_____

_____

_____

_____

_____

_____

_____

D = Discuss: What aspects of your refined concept need further investigation? What problems could arise? From whom else do you need input? How will a new approach (form, program, team, etc.) benefit the organization? What will it cost (in terms of both time and money)? What other questions do you need to raise before the concept is finalized and then implemented?

_____

_____

_____

_____

_____

_____

_____

_____

PROMOTION ACTIVITY #15:

Connect with a famous person.

This prestige ploy is not as hard as you might think, but it demands two things: sincerity and preparation. While it's true that famous people are busy people, it is also true that many of them are eager to "give back"—to their communities, to the less fortunate, to those sincerely interested in their field. Contacting a famous person just so you can say you have had that contact is a waste of everyone's time. But contacting a famous person whose advice you sincerely seek can be profitable on many levels.

This is where the preparation comes in. You will have to think of an individual who is prominent in your field or perhaps someone whose fame cuts across several fields. If the person has written a book, you can send him or her a letter in care of the publisher. (Your local librarian can provide the addresses of publishers.) If the individual heads a large organization, you can, of course, send a note to that address. Few famous people operate in a vacuum—if they are leading others, there is a place where they can be reached.

As you draft your letter, keep uppermost in your mind the cardinal sin that can be committed in a famous/not-so-famous person relationship: wasting the famous person's time. Keep your letter short. Keep it clear and to the point. Do not write more than three lines about yourself. Instead, write down one or two specific questions you would like to have the famous person answer. You may also ask for advice about an idea you are proposing.

When the response arrives, cite this authoritative individual as a further reason for moving forward with your plan. To increase the likelihood of connectedness with a famous person, contact more than one.

 PROMOTION ACTIVITY #16:

Coin a memorable phrase.

In many workplaces, employees post clever sayings on bulletin boards or on the walls of workstations. You've seen them:

- "If God had had a secretary, the world would have been created in *five* days."
- "Be it ever so humbling, there is no place like work."
- "The difficult we can do immediately. The impossible will take a little longer."
- "If an hour has been spent amending a sentence, someone will move to delete the paragraph."
- "Any clean surface in this office has a life expectancy of two minutes."
- "Ginger Rogers did everything Fred Astaire did, but she did it backwards and in high heels." —Faith Whittlesey

How to think of a witticism is the task before you. Try some of these techniques:

- Begin as some of the previous examples did—with an "If…" sentence.
- Try putting a new twist on an existing saying. "Be it ever so humble, there is no place like home" becomes "Be it ever so humbling, there is no place like work."
- Notice things around you, such as how quickly a clean desk becomes piled with papers, and make a wry observation.

Once you have your maxim in hand, let others hear it (at meetings, at coffee breaks) and see it (e-mail, a little sign on your desk, a filler for the company newsletter), but always make sure your name is attached to the clever remark. If you are especially gifted with this kind of verbal flexibility, you may wish to put out a whole book of these puns. (You could title it *The Pun Also Rises*.)

PROMOTION ACTIVITY #17:

Help others with something you are not expected to help with.

Look around you. Who is new to the organization or lacks experience with a particular assignment? What teams are undertaking some major projects? What committee has been formed to handle some special task such as the company picnic or the upcoming Christmas party? What group is planning a special occasion such as National Quality Month (in October) or National Secretaries Month (in April) or Black History Month (in February)?

This recommendation does not involve a long-term commitment. Instead, find a way to serve in an ex-officio capacity. Discover some small way that you can provide assistance to others who never would have thought of asking you for it. Take a new employee to lunch her first week so you can "explain the ropes." Offer to accept calls while an important meeting is going on.

If you have a special skill, offer to share it with others. For example, if you know calligraphy, you could offer to sign certificates. If you have a statistics background, you could offer to look over analyzed data before they are forwarded to management. Bring in doughnuts on the day your colleagues may be making an important presentation to management or to an influential client. On a more personal note, offer to babysit one night for someone whose relative is in the hospital.

Most people do not forget kindnesses. And if you are genuinely interested in helping others in ways they do not expect, you'll find a positive return on your investment: others will show appreciation, you'll enhance your reputation, and others will see new dimensions of your personality.

Power

2

Power! Many people view it from a negative perspective. They associate it with the words "abuse of." To be "power-hungry" is to be viewed as controlling, manipulative, even megalomanic. And yet, if leaders did not have a drive for power, they would be unable to win wars, to move corporations toward mission-accomplishment, to develop programs to put astronauts in outer space. Without power—the ability to achieve success by directing the efforts of others—very little would ever get done.

There is nothing wrong with increasing your power base—as long as your reason for doing so is ethical. But when the rationale behind the power acquisition is less than honorable, then both individuals and organizations will find trouble, not triumph, at the end of their mission.

Before reading this section on ways to increase the power you already have, briefly answer the following questions.

- How would you define "power"?_____

_____

_____

_____

- How much power do you already have? _____

_____

_____

- Why would you like more?_____

_____

_____

- What will you do with more? _____

_____

_____

- Who in your organization has the kind of power you would like to have? ____

_____

_____

- How does that person use his or her power? _____

_____

_____

- What are the various types of power?_____

_____

_____

• Why are others drawn to people with power? _____

_____

_____

• What, in your opinion, constitutes an abuse of power? _____

_____

_____

_____

_____

_____

_____

_____

To learn more about your power potential, answer check "T" for true or "F" for false for each of the following statements.

T   F

☐ ☐ 1. I like being in charge of things.

☐ ☐ 2. I enjoy taking responsibility.

☐ ☐ 3. Decision-making is a process I enjoy.

☐ ☐ 4. I am comfortable with delegating tasks to others.

☐ ☐ 5. I am comfortable settling disputes between two people.

☐ ☐ 6. I enjoy long-range planning.

☐ ☐ 7. I am effective in getting others to support our mission.

☐ ☐ 8. I like setting a direction and helping others follow it.

☐ ☐ 9. People listen to my ideas and usually accept and implement them.

☐ ☐ 10. I view myself as a leader.

If you answered "true" to seven or more of these questions, you are probably the sort of person who understands the benefits of power and is comfortable exploring them.

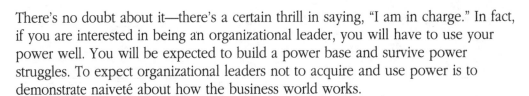

There's no doubt about it—there's a certain thrill in saying, "I am in charge." In fact, if you are interested in being an organizational leader, you will have to use your power well. You will be expected to build a power base and survive power struggles. To expect organizational leaders not to acquire and use power is to demonstrate naiveté about how the business world works.

Research shows that the most effective leaders are those who effectively make decisions for others to carry out, those who lower resistance to change.

According to Peter G. Stone, vice president/finance and law for Ottaway Newspapers, Inc., here are some keys to keep in mind if you are a leader introducing change, particularly at a group level:

- Keep "the players" involved.
- Brainstorm and role-play to develop various scenarios of the change and the consequences and results of each scenario.
- Continually stimulate teamwork and self-esteem.
- Offer encouragement.
- Provide recognition and rewards for successful performance.
- Have fun.

Stone also discusses the ethical stance required of leaders who effect change and thus exert a positive power:

> I stand up for my beliefs, am outspoken, and believe that boldness in action brings about change. I am not dogmatic and find a certain truth in whatever works best—don't interpret this to mean that the ends justify the means. I am a total skeptic and probably question too much. I like to think my consuming curiosity will lead to a better ultimate course of action.

Study the answers you wrote on the last few pages. Are you the sort of person who is comfortable with power? Not everyone is. But if you are, this section will suggest several ways you can attain success by directing the efforts of others.

PROMOTION ACTIVITY #18:

Raise your "likability" level.

Chief executives in a *Wall Street Journal*/Gallup Organization poll were asked what it takes to get ahead. Not surprisingly, 32 percent of the CEOs in 282 of the country's largest firms identified the ability to get along with others, ranking it second behind integrity, which came in at 36 percent. CEOs in 300 medium-sized firms—36 percent of them—ranked the ability to get along with others as the number one way to get ahead.

Of course, getting ahead today may not mean what it meant a generation ago. Today, there are more managers than there are management jobs. And so getting ahead may mean being given a new opportunity or being put in charge of a special project instead of getting a promotion. However it is defined, though, getting ahead generally means having more power.

Let's assume these CEOs are correct in believing that your people skills will help advance your career and thus increase your power. Would you describe yourself as the consummate people-person? If not, you could probably raise your likability level. (Most of us can.) Try the self-assessment on the next page to find out which of your interpersonal skills you could improve.

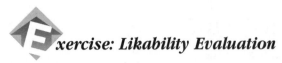

Exercise: Likability Evaluation

Here are some of the traits commonly associated with personal power. Score yourself on a scale of 1 (low) to 10 (high) on each of these traits. Don't over-analyze yourself. Rather, do a quick self-assessment. Instead of tallying your score, concentrate on the areas where you scored "5" or lower.

Trait	Score
Ability to influence	1 • • • 5 • • • 10 _____
Self-confidence	1 • • • 5 • • • 10 _____
Likability	1 • • • 5 • • • 10 _____
Networking skills	1 • • • 5 • • • 10 _____
Self-confidence	1 • • • 5 • • • 10 _____
Trustworthiness	1 • • • 5 • • • 10 _____
Ability to return favors	1 • • • 5 • • • 10 _____
Expertise	1 • • • 5 • • • 10 _____
Ability to help others advance their careers	1 • • • 5 • • • 10 _____
Sincerity	1 • • • 5 • • • 10 _____

Record here what you can do to raise your scores in the areas where you scored below "5." _____

_____

_____

_____

_____

_____

_____

_____

_____

In which one area did you score lowest or would you most like to improve?

_____

_____

_____

_____

Write the dialog you would use in the following situation: A co-worker whom you barely know has approached you and asked that you serve as her mentor. Your first inclination is to say "no" because you have heard this young woman has a reputation as a troublemaker. On the other hand, you are genuinely interested in helping others, especially young people. How would you respond? Your dialog should reflect the trait (listed above) you are trying to improve.

_____

_____

_____

_____

_____

_____

_____

_____

_____

_____

_____

_____

_____

PROMOTION ACTIVITY #19:

Acquire expert power.

No matter who you are, there is something you know how to do exceedingly well. That something may or may not be related to your job. Self-promoters have learned how to take their expert knowledge and use it to increase their power.

Let's say, for example, that you coach Little Leaguers. As a result, you have learned a number of things about motivation, about winning, about losing, about the ways people work together. You can apply this learning to the workplace, where you can coach a team or conduct a lunchtime lecture about maintaining momentum or developing team spirit.

Or, you might enjoy gourmet cooking. If you look beyond the actual baking and basting, you will discover things you have learned about yourself—things like creativity, receptivity to new ideas, the ability to organize and entertain, the delicacies of foreign countries, and so forth. These are things you could easily put to good use in certain corporate circumstances.

Use the following questionnaire to help you think about ways you can use your knowledge in a specific area to increase your power.

Exercise: Knowledge Questionnaire

Assessing Your Current Expertise

1. What do you know a lot about? _____

2. What specific skills have you learned as a result of your involvement in this area?

   _____

   _____

   _____

   _____

   _____

   _____

3. What skills does the organization value? _____

   _____

   _____

   _____

   _____

4. How could you align the skills you possess with the skills your organization values?

   _____

   _____

   _____

   _____

5. How could you make your boss aware of the valuable skills you possess?

   _____

   _____

   _____

   _____

Acquiring Additional Expertise

1. What trends are developing in the general business world and in your particular industry? What recent or upcoming legislation/court decisions could have a powerful impact on your firm?

_____

_____

_____

_____

_____

_____

_____

_____

_____

_____

2. Which of these interest you enough to make you develop expert knowledge about them?

_____

_____

_____

_____

_____

_____

_____

_____

_____

_____

_____

3. (a) For which of the following skills, commonly regarded as essential for workplace success, would you rate yourself above average?
   - Problem-solving
   - Writing
   - Time management
   - Speaking
   - Training
   - Interviewing
   - Teamwork
   - Computer literacy

   _____

   _____

   _____

   _____

   _____

   _____

   _____

   _____

   (b) In which areas would you rate yourself less than average? What are you doing to improve your skills in these areas?

   _____

   _____

   _____

   _____

   _____

   _____

   _____

PROMOTION ACTIVITY #20:

Acquire power through association.

Sometimes people acquire power by associating with others who have a great deal more power. The secretary to the company president, for instance, has a distinct power due to her relationship with the president.

Who in your organization enjoys extensive power? How did they acquire this power? Because of their position? Expertise? Popularity? Ability to persuade? It is certainly possible for you to form a friendly relationship with one or more of the individuals who have power in your organization.

Use the following chart to help you determine how to get the attention of others who are powerful. Keep in mind, however, that the purpose of establishing the relationship isn't just to "use" the person. Consider what you have to offer to the relationship in order to make it reciprocal. While this person may be able to loosen bottlenecks or connect you with others who can help you achieve your goals, be prepared to open a door or two for that person as well.

Exercise: Powerful Association Possibilities

1. Name of powerful person _____

   Kind of power _____

   How well you know the person   1 • • • 5 • • • 10 (high)

   Likelihood of establishing a friendly relationship   1 • • • 5 • • • 10 (high)

2. Name of powerful person _____

   Kind of power _____

   How well you know the person   1 • • • 5 • • • 10 (high)

   Likelihood of establishing a friendly relationship   1 • • • 5 • • • 10 (high)

3. Name of powerful person _____

   Kind of power _____

   How well you know the person   1 • • • 5 • • • 10 (high)

   Likelihood of establishing a friendly relationship   1 • • • 5 • • • 10 (high)

4. Name of powerful person _____

   Kind of power _____

   How well you know the person   1 • • • 5 • • • 10 (high)

   Likelihood of establishing a friendly relationship   1 • • • 5 • • • 10 (high)

How will you form your relationship with the person who rated a high score on "likelihood of establishing a friendly relationship"? What do you have in common? What could you offer that would benefit the person? Plan a strategy and execute it. The worst that can happen, after all, is that someone will decline your invitation to lunch.

_____

_____

_____

_____

_____

_____

PROMOTION ACTIVITY #21:

Become a knowledge broker.

Knowledge is power. The more knowledge you have, the more power you will have. But in addition to having it, you must share it. And there's the "rub," so to speak. You will have to maintain a delicate balance—providing pertinent information but not so much that you become a pest or develop a reputation for being a "know-it-all."

When you share knowledge, you are operating from a win-win position. The recipient will appreciate receiving valuable information, and you will be appreciated as the source of up-to-the-minute knowledge.

One way to decide who should have what information is to learn the special interests of various people you would like to impress or to whom you would like to extend a favor. The best way to obtain this information is to listen carefully and note their special hobbies or subjects they want to know more about.

A word to the wise: Avoid the appearance of "buttering up the higher-ups." Colleagues who are not part of your information loop may regard your actions as manipulative. Should someone accuse you of this, tell that person you are a voracious reader and simply enjoy sharing the information you run across. Inquire about that person's interests and promise to send articles on those topics his or her way. Keep your promise.

Exercise: Information Ledger

1. Whom do you consider the most interesting, most powerful, or most influential individuals in your organization?

   Name _____

   Article title _____ Date sent_____

   Response_____

   Name _____

   Article title _____ Date sent_____

   Response_____

   Name _____

   Article title _____ Date sent_____

   Response_____

   Name _____

   Article title _____ Date sent_____

   Response_____

2. Acquire as much information as you can about each person's interests. Consider:
   - Where do they go for vacation?
   - What hobbies do they have?
   - What are their favorite sports teams?
   - What type of reading do they enjoy?
   - Who are their heroes?
   - What types of things do they collect?
   - What industry-specific topics are they concerned with?
   - What conferences do they attend each year?
   - Others?

3. Use the above ledger to keep track of the people to whom you send articles and their response to your knowledge-brokering efforts. If you don't receive a favorable response within a month of your second submission, quit sharing the articles with that person.

PROMOTION ACTIVITY #22:

Assume leadership of a project.

By "strutting your leadership stuff" you will increase your chances of being asked to lead a project. You may have to serve as a self-appointed leader of the first project but—assuming it is successful—you will be able to catch the eye of the higher-ups who make decisions about who will be put in charge of future projects.

What project should you undertake? The possibilities are endless. You may wish to designate one day as company-wide "clean out the files" day. You might organize a potluck luncheon or a retirement party. You could raise funds for a worthy cause or begin a company fitness program.

Use the silhouettes below to start your creative juices flowing. Select one that seems to beckon you, and then answer the questions on the next page about it.

Exercise: Your Leadership Project

1. Why do you think you selected what you did?

_____

_____

_____

_____

2. What kind of project possibilities does it inspire in you?

_____

_____

_____

_____

3. Select one and tell how it would benefit the company.

_____

_____

_____

4. How much of your time would it take? On whom would you have to depend to carry out this project? Whose approval would you need?

_____

_____

_____

5. How could accomplishing this project increase your personal power?

_____

_____

_____

_____

6. If the project is not one that would enhance your professional image, select another and answer the same questions about it.

PROMOTION ACTIVITY #23:

Use the grapevine to your advantage.

It's impossible to kill the corporate grapevine. No matter how often the tendrils are chopped, new ones sprout in other places while the old ones grow at weed-speed. Although it often wastes enormous amounts of time, the grapevine can be a positive force in an organization. In fact, you can use the power of the grapevine to increase your own power. Used judiciously, both you and your company can profit.

You can advise others of your capabilities, your special talent, the unique contributions you can make. Use the worksheet on the next page to set some goals. Then, as you accomplish your goals, let others know. Each month, you should inform different people—in a professional, non-boastful way—of what you accomplished that month beyond the requirements of your job. The word about your skills will soon spread through the grapevine.

Remember, power is typically considered the ability to get things done by obtaining the resources needed to turn a vision into reality. As others learn about your capabilities, they will be more willing to allocate resources to you—including human resources.

Exercise: Seeds to Be Planted for the Grapevine

On the notepad below, record the most outstanding thing you do each month—ideally something that is related to the work you or your company does. Also record the names of people who should know about this talent. Try to make the information-receivers different people each month.

January   *February*   *March*   *April*

May   *June*   *July*   *August*

September   *October*   *November*   *December*

PROMOTION ACTIVITY #24:

Safely disobey ... or at least disagree.

"Never use the excuse of following orders," Roger Meade tells us, "as the rationale for following a poor course of action." His advice is truer today, in these "nanosecond nineties," than ever before. We are living in chaotic times, when old prescriptions for success no longer work.

In today's business world, filled with paradoxes and rife with status-quo contradictions, the old definitions of loyalty are being reconstructed. Loyalty now means doing what's in the best interests of the organization. It used to mean doing what was in the best interests of the boss, who may or may not have had the best interests of the organization in mind.

With reinvention and reengineering forcing us to rethink, most employers appreciate the employee with fresh insights, with nonconformist thinking. Those who insist on being "yes" men and "yes" women are going "no" where.

The new attitude is evident in the response of a job applicant who was seeking employment with a Fortune 500 company. The interviewer asked the familiar "tell-me-about-yourself" question. The applicant replied, "I think you should know I consider myself a non-conforming conformist."

The interviewer's interest was piqued. "Please explain that," he requested.

The applicant happily did so. "I will conform to the policies and procedures, the job requirements, the typical expectations you have for a person in this position. However, if I am ever asked to do something I consider unethical or contrary to the corporate mission, I won't conform."

Oh, yes. She did get the job, in part because of her refreshingly honest answer. She took a risk in being so open. Yes, it might have backfired. But employers concerned about the good of the company will not overlook the good in a person who is so candid. A word of warning: If you intend to engage in similar mild-to-moderate risks, think seriously about the degree of diplomacy they require. Some people who disagree put their jobs in jeopardy because of the way they express or time their disagreement. Others, however, can disagree in a way that makes listeners receptive to new possibilities.

Polish your persuasion skills before attempting a "disobedient" stance. Diplomatic defiance will certainly increase your reputation and the likelihood that others will listen to your ideas. Less-than-diplomatic defiance, though, can label you as a rebel or an upstart, as someone who is defiant and unconcerned about the organizational mission.

Tom Peters boldly states, "If you have gone a whole week without being disobedient, you are doing yourself and your organization a disservice." Before you begin radically altering your behavior, however, engage in some introspection. Use the forms on the next pages to help you determine your willingness to disagree when necessary and your ability to be powerfully persuasive without being offensive.

Self-Assessment: How Well Do I Take an Independent Stance?

Directions: For each statement, place an "X" on the continuum to represent how often you take an independent stance.

1. I speak up at meetings.	1 • • • 5 • • • 10
2. I take an unpopular position.	1 • • • 5 • • • 10
3. I disagree with my boss as needed.	1 • • • 5 • • • 10
4. I propose ideas.	1 • • • 5 • • • 10
5. I influence others.	1 • • • 5 • • • 10
6. I play devil's advocate.	1 • • • 5 • • • 10
7. I "hold my own."	1 • • • 5 • • • 10
8. I use facts to make decisions.	1 • • • 5 • • • 10
9. I take charge of my own destiny.	1 • • • 5 • • • 10
10. I have established goals.	1 • • • 5 • • • 10

Scoring: Tally your score now. If it is 70 or higher, commend yourself on being an independent thinker. If your score is lower, build your confidence by engaging more often in the actions listed in this assessment.

What was your lowest score? _____

What is holding you back? What is preventing you from acting more independently, more assertively in this regard? _____

_____

_____

_____

How can you overcome those restraining forces? _____

_____

_____

_____

Self-Assessment: How Persuasive Am I?

Directions: Write the item number for each persuasive technique listed below in the corner of the hexagon that most accurately reflects your mastery of the technique.

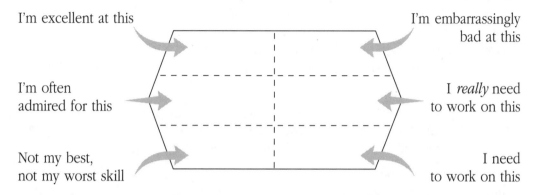

I'm excellent at this

I'm embarrassingly bad at this

I'm often admired for this

I *really* need to work on this

Not my best, not my worst skill

I need to work on this

1. I find that people really listen when I speak.

2. I consciously decide how, when, and where to communicate (speak or write) information others may not want to know about.

3. I anticipate objections and have rebuttals ready.

4. I use precedents to strengthen my position.

5. I use statistics to support the points I am making.

6. I think about what may be offensive to others and strive to avoid such references in my communications.

7. I do not waste people's time by saying things that don't need to be said.

8. I make an effort to align important messages with the organizational mission.

9. I take into account the listening/learning styles of those who will receive my message.

10. I answer the WIFM question ("What's in it for me?") before I address an audience.

Scoring: Do half or more of your numbers fall on the left-hand side of the hexagon? If so, you are well on your way to being a persuasive communicator. If not, you need more practice with the techniques whose numbers fall on the right-hand side.

PROMOTION ACTIVITY #25:

Carpe diem—"seize the day" . . . or the opportunity.

It's easy to complain. It's harder, and no doubt nobler, to look around and recognize the many things we have to be grateful for. In *Uh-Oh,* author Robert Fulghum describes Sigmund Wollman, an Auschwitz survivor. After listening to Fulghum complain about food, Wollman told him: "If you break your neck, if you have nothing to eat, if your house is on fire—then you got a problem. Everything else is inconvenience."

All around you are opportunities for excellence, problems waiting to be transformed into solutions. All they need is the right person with the right attitude. You have the power to be the alchemist who can transmute the negative to a positive.

To illustrate, think about one area in particular—training. Many employees enter the training site grumbling and mumbling—they'd rather be anywhere than in a classroom exposed to new knowledge for a full day. And yet, in that classroom, lie uncountable opportunities to excel.

Read how employees at the Port Hueneme Division of the Naval Surface Warfare Center in Virginia Beach view team training (see box). They've taken the new skills they learned as a team and applied them to other areas of their lives. They saw an opportunity to improve themselves and they seized it—not only to achieve job-related goals but personal ones as well.

Opportunity to Excel...

By Colette Knight, Debra E. Kelly, Charmaine Savage, Amelia S. Osmunson, Dante R. Acedo, Glynn Bashford, Lorraine J. Kittel, Linda L. Webb, Terry G. Sellers, Nancy C. Konstantinidis, Avis Z. Fluke, Brenda T. Zettervall, Kimberly S. Skurow, Jerald A. Kendall, Rance Maddox, Linda Sifford, and Glen Washburn

Quality Improvement concepts provide the educational opportunity to synthesize the experiences and observations of others. The challenge is to use this education to create opportunities for effective communication and behavior modification.

Lack of effective communication is often the number one cause for a team's lack of success. Some of the tools for effective communication include preparing meeting agendas, maintaining accurate public records, and establishing goals and ground rules.

The concepts, tools, and methods learned for better communications can result in behavior changes that will alter the course of our lives. We can now boast of our ability in improved presentation skills, problem-solving, and interpersonal relations.

Education—whether formal or self-attained—has enabled a new dawn to break within each of us. Our changed behavior has enabled us to deal with any and all—from storekeepers to presidents. We must give a large percentage of credit to the famed gurus—Deming, Juran, and Crosby—but the greatest credit goes to ourselves.

Lee Iacocca has noted that "in the end, all business operations can be reduced to three words: people, product, and profits. People come first. Unless you've got a good team, you can't do much with the other two." A good team must be educated and given the opportunity to use skills and techniques they've learned. Applying Quality Improvement training techniques greatly improves education and creates opportunities for self-improvement, behavior modification, and better communication skills. These skills promote increased individual contributions to the organization while concurrently broadening personal horizons. Team tools and techniques properly applied benefit the individual as well as the organization.

xercise: Problem or Inconvenience?

Directions: As quickly as you can, make a list of twenty problems you are facing this week. The problems can deal with your work, your job, your family, your relationships, your goals, your health—any aspect of your life.

1. _____ _____

2. _____ _____

3. _____ _____

4. _____ _____

5. _____ _____

6. _____ _____

7. _____ _____

8. _____ _____

9. _____ _____

10. _____ _____

11. _____ _____

12. _____ _____

13. _____ _____

14. _____ _____

15. _____ _____

16. _____ _____

17. _____ _____

18. _____ _____

19. _____ _____

20. _____ _____

In the space to the right of your list, write the letters "Cr" to indicate a critical problem, "Co" to indicate a problem you can cope with, and "In" to indicate a problem that is really just an inconvenience. Reevaluate those you indicated to be critical ("Cr"), using this criterion: "Compared to having a loved one die in a plane crash or to finding out you have a life-threatening illness, how critical is this problem?" Use a scale of 1 to 5, with 5 meaning "most critical." Now, think of ways you can turn these problems into opportunities. Realize that sometimes the opportunity doesn't reside in the solution. It lies in getting there—the new skills you develop, the new people you meet, the fears you conquer as you move toward resolution of both problems and inconveniences.

PROMOTION ACTIVITY #26:

Fill your personal portfolio with glowing recommendations.

If you are reading this book, you must be interested in promoting yourself. One of the most impressive ways to do that is to keep a personal portfolio of glowing recommendations. Then, when you are in line for a promotion or when you have left the company and are seeking employment elsewhere, you can show your portfolio each time someone asks to see those references that are "available on request."

While you can certainly overdo this, the truth is that the average person *under*does it. Most people have a resumé and perhaps a list of references a prospective employer or client can contact, but few have taken the time to amass testimonials about their capabilities. Just as the author of a book seeks endorsements from other authors, you can and should be collecting commendations from those who have worked with you and who know what you can do. (A sample letter requesting a letter of reference is shown on the next page.)

A note of caution here: You must be careful not to create the impression that you are developing your personal portfolio because you are planning to leave the company. Explain carefully, as the following letter does, that you are merely seeking evaluations from various people to ready yourself for the next promotion, should it come your way.

Certainly, your self-confidence will increase as you gather this ambition-ammunition. And your readiness for your next position of power will be immeasurably enhanced.

Exercise: Sample Letter Requesting Recommendation

Using the letter below as a model, compose a letter that requests recommendations about your job performance and abilities.

Dear Susan:

As you may remember from our discussions, I hope to be considered for the next promotional opportunity that becomes available. To that end, I am preparing a personal portfolio with letters of reference from people who have worked with me and who can attest to my abilities.

I would certainly appreciate such an endorsement from you concerning my knowledge and skills, especially as they relate to the work we did together on _____(name of project or team)_____.

Your schedule is a busy one, I know, but if I could have the letter within the next two weeks I would appreciate it very much. Thank you in advance for your support.

Sincerely,

_____

Your Name

_____

_____

_____

_____

_____

_____

_____

_____

_____

PROMOTION ACTIVITY #27:

Blow your own horn: make a radio or television appearance.

The average American city has several radio and television stations. Think about the possibilities they provide for self-promotion. Think, too, about how eager they are to find—every single day—interesting people who can engage their audiences.

Do you have something that could interest others? Of course you do! We all do. That something, though, may not yet be refined enough to be presented before live audiences.

Use the questions below to help you decide what might be an interesting topic. The worksheet on the next page will help you get that topic in shape for its media debut. Then take a deep breath and call your local stations to ask about the procedures for being interviewed on one of their talk or news programs.

- On what topic could you be considered an expert?
- When do you find you are best received by others? (For example, when you are talking about computers? When you are sharing an anecdote? When you are expressing your views on a controversial subject?)
- On what topic have you done extensive reading?
- If you were going to write a book, what would be its theme?
- What do you feel most passionate about?
- What interesting discoveries have you made lately?
- What do people usually compliment you on?
- If you could give a speech on any subject, what would you choose?
- Is there anything in your background that relates to a topic of current local interest?

Exercise: Media Worksheet

Use this worksheet to help you logically present your topic to the media.

1. *Introduction:* What "hook" could you use to initially intrigue the audience? Is there a story, a quotation, an anecdote, a humorous incident, or a fascinating statistic you could use to capture your audience's attention?

2. *Body:* Here you have to substantiate your story or topic. What essential points will you make? How can you validate them? What statistics do you have to demonstrate the extent of the problem or the frequency of the event? What do the experts have to say about the subject? What recent books or newspaper articles have been written?

   If your presentation is more personal—such as two family members being reunited after twenty years—how can you make your experience relevant for others in the audience?

3. *Conclusion:* Again, think of a hook that will leave your audience wanting more. Is there an encompassing quotation, a relevant bit of history, a famous person association, an expensive precedent, or future promise you can end with? Plan a memorable conclusion.

In all likelihood, your appearance will be an interview as opposed to a five-minute presentation that would permit a logical flow of important points. So, you must anticipate the questions the program host or reporter will ask you. Write the questions here. Then try to write answers that get to the point quickly and deliver the message you want the audience to hear. (Ask friends and family members to help you create additional questions.)

_____

_____

_____

_____

_____

_____

_____

_____

PROMOTION ACTIVITY #28:

Climb a symbolically big mountain, at least once a year.

The symbol of a mountain is an appropriate one for individuals seeking to promote themselves. Think about the powerful people in your organization or in your community. What do they do that demonstrates their power? (This is not an easy task.) Your initial responses may be "hold a press conference," "fly first class," "vacation on the French Riviera," "make tough decisions, or "play golf with powerful people." But keep on thinking. Focus on their accomplishments, on ideas they've been able to push through or changes they've been able to implement. The more items you can list on the following lines, the better:

_____

_____

_____

_____

_____

_____

_____

_____

_____

_____

_____

_____

_____

_____

_____

_____

Now turn to the Accomplishment Analysis worksheet on the next page and do more hard thinking, this time about your own accomplishments.

Exercise: Accomplishment Analysis

1. Which of your accomplishments in the last twelve months are you proudest of?

_____

_____

_____

2. Which lifetime challenges have you met most successfully? Which ones brought you the greatest satisfaction when you achieved them? _____

_____

_____

_____

_____

3. Beside each of the items you listed in questions 1 and 2, draw either a little mountain or a big mountain.

4. Of all the power gestures you listed on the preceding page, which ones do you feel you could do yourself?

_____

_____

_____

_____

5. Having thought about your answers to the previous four questions, select one power-gesture, one big-mountain action you could undertake in the next six months that would demonstrate your personal power. Pledge to perform that action.

_____

_____

_____

_____

_____

PROMOTION ACTIVITY #29:

Write your own declaration of independence.

The people who are the most cheated are the ones who cheat themselves. We cheat ourselves in many ways—one way is not realizing our full potential. As H. G. Wells observed, the only true measure of success is the ratio between what we might have been and what we have become. The lower the ratio, the more successful we can declare ourselves.

You must lessen the gap between what you might become and what you are.

If you're like most people, you haven't even begun to fully explore the power of your unique essence. (Even Einstein estimated he was using only 25 percent of his mental powers.) There is so much more you can do—no matter how much you have already done. But determining what your ratio currently is and then deciding to make it lower requires serious introspection. Be forewarned: some of that introspection will make you uncomfortable. But the discomfort is usually what moves us to action.

The word *potential* is derived from the Latin word *potens,* which means "power." To discover your fullest powers, to uncover your latent potential, you must define and then eliminate the barriers that prevent you from being the best you.

Dependencies are some of those barriers. Whether they are physical, mental, or emotional, each of us has things or people we depend on. Some of the dependencies—such as solid friendships—are healthy. Others have a negative impact on our lives. If we are dependent on cigarettes, for example, we are preventing ourselves from reaching the potential of a healthy body.

The form on the next page will help you sort out the healthy from the unhealthy dependencies in your life. After determining which ones you need to eliminate, you should be able to write your declaration of personal independence.

Exercise: Declaration of Personal Independence

1. What might you realistically become?

_____

_____

_____

_____

_____

2. List here all the people and things you depend on. Beside each item you list, write the letter "H" to indicate a healthy dependency or the letter "U" to indicate an unhealthy one. Then write the letter "P" beside the items that will most help you transform what you have become into what you can still become.

_____

_____

_____

_____

_____

_____

_____

_____

_____

_____

3. Draft your Declaration of Personal Independence now. Choose one way in which you can declare your freedom from some dependency. Resolve to become independent within the next six months. Once your draft is done, ask for input from those who are close to you. Prepare a final statement and post it near your desk or on your bathroom mirror, someplace where you'll see it often.

PROMOTION ACTIVITY #30:

Appear and act like a power player.

Believers in the self-fulfilling prophecy know that we can become what we imagine ourselves to be. If you truly wish to become a power player, you must evince the appearance and actions that are commonly associated with powerful figures. The problem is that different people have different definitions of which appearances and actions spell power. There are some commonalties, of course, but the definition you will live with is the definition you create based on your observations, your reading, your discussions, your experience.

The following exercises will help you develop your own definition of power looks and power behaviors.

 **_xercise: Power Player Quiz_**

1. Name three powerful people you know or know of.

   - _____
   - _____
   - _____

2. Describe the way these individuals look.

   - _____
   - _____
   - _____

   What similarities do they share? _____

   _____

   _____

   _____

   _____

   _____

3. Describe the way these individuals act around others.

   - _____
   - _____
   - _____

   What similarities do they share? _____

   _____

   _____

   _____

   _____

   _____

4. Based on your responses to questions 1 to 3, define the "look of power." The explain how you can incorporate (more of) that look into your own style.

_____

_____

_____

_____

_____

_____

_____

Exercise: The Look of Power Quiz

A. Directions: Listed below are quotations related to power. Place a check mark in front of those you agree with or that make sense to you.

1. _____ "Improve your ability to make good first impressions." (Jack Horn)

2. _____ "Power is self-reverence, self-knowledge, self-control." (Alfred Lord Tennyson)

3. _____ "Power is the ability to get people to do what you want them to—and the ability to resist being forced to do what you don't want to do." (Mitchell J. Posner)

4. _____ "I suspect that a large number of managers perform significantly below their potential because they do not understand the dynamics of power and because they have not nurtured and developed the instincts needed to effectively acquire and use power." (John Kotter)

5. _____ "Dress as if you were a more senior executive than you actually are." (Jack Horn)

6. _____ "Wait until they hurt you twice before you strike back." (Michael Doyle and William Perkins)

7. _____ "Defining what you are after is 50 percent of the battle in getting there." (Charles J. Givens)

8. _____ "Powerlessness is a state of mind. If you think you're powerless, you are." (Tom Peters)

9. _____ "Analyze an adversary's tactics and use whatever might work for you." (Jeffrey P. Davidson)

10. _____ "Spend the extra money . . . buy good shoes." (John M. Capozzi)

11. _____ "You need to pay attention not only to the messages you send, but also the messages you receive." (National Institute of Business Management)

12. _____ "For innovators, power is the ability to create wealth by organizing and motivating people." (Michael Maccoby)

13. _____ "All power is trust." (Benjamin Disraeli)

B. The statements below are paraphrases of the famous quotations on the preceding page. In the blank before each statement, write a number—either 0, 5, or 10—to indicate how closely you resemble or possess the power description or trait mentioned.

0 = Never

5 = Sometimes

10 = Always

1. _____ I make good first impressions on people.

2. _____ I respect myself.

_____ I know myself.

_____ I have self-control.

3. _____ People do what I want them to.

_____ I resist doing things I don't want to do.

4. _____ I understand the dynamics of power.

_____ I have worked to develop my "power instincts."

5. _____ My attire resembles what people above me wear rather than the way people at my current level dress.

6. _____ I will retaliate if I have been wronged but only after I'm certain there was a direct attack made on me.

7. _____ My goals are written down.

8. _____ I believe I am a powerful person.

9. _____ I have studied the power tactics of both those who support me and those who oppose me.

10. _____ My wardrobe looks as if I have invested time, money, and effort.

11. _____ I am a good communicator.

_____ I pay attention to body language.

12. _____ I can organize and motivate others.

13. _____ Other people trust me.

Obviously, the higher your score, the more you are aware of your own power and of how to use it for positive purposes.

PROMOTION ACTIVITY #31:

Work with the human resources department.

"Human resources departments will become more powerful in the 1990s. Succession planning and management development will become top priorities as companies continue to slim down. They have to get smarter about their bench strength." So says Dr. Mary Anne Devanna, research director of Columbia University's Management Institute and director of Executive Education at Columbia's School of Business.

Her words are echoed by author Tom Jackson, who observes that there is "an aching need for those who can get the job done in creating work-ready employees." Formally or informally, internally or externally, you can do your share to create "work-ready employees." Your efforts will no doubt be appreciated and your power will grow as others recognize your contribution and come to depend on you for repeat performances.

To begin, contact the human resources department in your organization. Explain that you are interested in learning more about training and that you would like to volunteer your services—perhaps once a week during your lunch hour or at the beginning or end of the day. By beginning informally, you will learn a great deal about what goes on in a corporate classroom. Even if your initial efforts focus on things like registration, name cards, or equipment needs, you will get a "behind-the-scenes" look at how training is conducted.

Given the cost of external trainers, the numerous responsibilities of the internal trainers, and the widely accepted Quality principle that "those who are closest to the process know it best," many organizations are asking employees to participate in the training process. Some organizations even pay their employees extra to teach after-hours classes!

Once you have gained enough experience (both behind-the-scenes and on-stage), you might even "take your show on the road" and expend your influence in the larger community. For example, local libraries, women's group, and volunteer organizations are always seeking interesting speakers. Of course, you will have to tailor your presentation for different audiences, but some topics—such as workplace literacy—will interest any audience.

The worksheet on the next page will assist you as your prepare your presentation.

Exercise: Presentation Worksheet

1. What is my topic? _____

2. How does it relate to our organizational mission? _____

_____

_____

3. What is my objective for this lesson? _____

_____

_____

4. What is the audience size? _____

5. How should the room be arranged? _____

6. What audiovisual equipment will I need? _____

_____

7. What materials, including handouts and transparencies, will I need? _____

_____

8. What is the procedure I will follow as I present this lesson? (List the steps in sequential order.) _____

_____

_____

_____

9. What points do I want or expect my audience to remember?

_____

_____

_____

10. How can I assess how well they grasped these essential points?

_____

_____

_____

PROMOTION ACTIVITY #32:

Develop your persuasion power.

Think about the individuals who have served as President of the United States. Think about what motivates them. It certainly isn't money—for while $200,000 a year is a hefty sum, it pales in comparison to the millions that corporation presidents or financiers earn. Certainly, there is prestige associated with the position, but most of all, positions like the presidency offer power—again defined as the ability to make things happen. The President is captain of a very large team whose success depends on both his vision and his ability to persuade. If he can influence others, including Congress, the media, and the voters, he is likely to see that vision become reality.

We each have a sphere of influence—definitely not as large as the President's, but large enough to get things done. Whether you are trying to persuade management to accept a proposal, trying to persuade colleagues to follow your leadership, or trying to persuade others to accept your point of view, each and every day you are reaching out to the hearts and minds (and maybe even pocketbooks) of others.

You *can* improve your persuasive abilities and, thus, your influence. The worksheet on the following page is a good place to begin assessing your persuasion quotient. Before you begin, though, think of a project, plan, or proposal you have that needs the support of others. Respond to the following statements with that project in mind.

Exercise: Persuasion Do's and Don'ts

Directions: In the blank space before each statement, write either "do" or "don't" to indicate whether it is a technique you should or should not use to communicate persuasively.

1. _____ concede, if appropriate.

2. _____ emphasize the buzzwords that the audience endorses.

3. _____ propose an idea that contradicts prevalent thinking.

4. _____ have data available to substantiate your points.

5. _____ embed negative information.

6. _____ anticipate objections and be ready to counter them.

7. _____ cite precedents, if possible.

8. _____ obtain endorsements from a respected authority in the field.

9. _____ mention that you have this support.

10. _____ use a metaphor to explain your central theme or a relevant point.

11. _____ determine the need for action before beginning.

12. _____ informally publicize your proposal before formally presenting it.

13. _____ informally publicize your proposal after formally presenting it.

14. _____ cite the rewards that those who support your idea will receive.

15. _____ obtain wide support for your plan.

16. _____ mention the wide support you already have.

17. _____ let yourself be seen as an authority as far as this plan is concerned.

18. _____ avoid mentioning earlier mistakes or failures.

19. _____ seek the input of others.

20. _____ promise that their input will be incorporated into the plan.

Answers: You should have written "do" beside each answer except the last. If you find yourself disagreeing with any of the answers, discuss with a co-worker the possible reasons for the answer given. Don't let up until you can find someone with a reasonable explanation for an answer with which you initially disagreed.

 PROMOTION ACTIVITY #33:

Attend a conference at least once a year and add at least ten contacts to your address/phone file.

"You're as good as your Rolodex," Tom Peters tells us. He equates this paper network with the "will to create your own job and abolish your sense of powerlessness." How do you fatten the size of your contact file? There's only one way: You must get out there and meet people.

Since you probably work five days a week, it will be difficult to meet business people outside your work environment. This means you have to get away from work to make some new acquaintances. What better way to do this than to attend a national conference?

There are thousands of trade associations in America—surely you will be able to find one that pertains to your field or industry. But if you can't find a relevant professional association, attend a seminar sponsored by a national seminar group. These companies offer a broad range of topics, so it should be easy to find one that interests you.

Try attending the seminar in a nearby city rather than in your own, if possible. Yes, it will be more inconvenient, but the contacts you can make will be quite valuable. You may be thinking of other barriers: the organization will not pay or you can't get a day off from work. These barriers are easily surmountable: pay for it yourself and use a vacation day to attend. Remember that the best investment you can ever make is in yourself. In addition to the knowledge you will acquire, you will have the opportunity to meet new friends, to connect with other professionals, and even to visit a new city.

Make certain, though, that you do not merely attend sessions and then return to your hotel room. Pledge to meet and exchange business cards with at least ten others while you are there. Keep your purpose in mind: to network—not to net-"eat" or net-"sleep" or net-"shop." Networking means working—working to meet strangers in the hope they will become acquaintances, associates, or possibly even friends.

Here is one example of the power that networking will bring you. A property manager in Los Angeles, along with her fellow managers, was given a special assignment by the boss: find ways to improve the existing lease agreement.

Relatively new to the field, she was reluctant to admit—to the boss or to the other managers—that she lacked the expertise to analyze and then alter the current document.

Instead, she turned to her Rolodex, called a business acquaintance in another city, and asked him to send her the leasing document he had signed when he occupied office space in a commercial property. By analyzing the two documents, she discovered some areas of difference and applied those differences to enhance her own company's lease agreement.

The kudos she received from her boss transformed her Rolodex from a functional piece of office equipment to her most prized possession.

PROMOTION ACTIVITY #34:

Stand out from the crowd.

In Harvey Mackay's *Sharkproof,* Sandra Lee Stuart tells of her decision to stand out from the crowd of job applicants for a position as a reporter on major newspapers:

> I took five twenty-dollar bills and cut each of them in jagged halves. I wrote to the editors of the five papers enclosing half of a bill. I told them that I realized they probably had no openings and were probably receiving hundreds of applications, but all I wanted was a little bit of their time. If they would only agree to have lunch with me, I would bring the other half of the twenty and pay.

Among the responses was one from Ben Bradlee, then editor of the *Washington Post* and now a United States senator. He passed the letter and the half of the bill on to a friend who hired her immediately—after being her guest at lunch, of course.

Is it risky to do something unorthodox in your efforts to increase your power? Yes. Could your gestures be misinterpreted? Yes. Might others view you as odd rather than creative? Yes. Is it worth it to try to stand out from others? Yes, yes, yes.

Weigh the alternatives. Examine the worst-case scenario: "What is the worst that could happen if I did this?" In Ms. Stuart's case, the worst that could have happened is the editors simply wouldn't respond and she wouldn't get the job at their papers. But she didn't have the job anyway so she really wasn't risking much (except twenty dollars).

Before embarking on your "stand-out-from-the-crowd" endeavor, discuss it with a trusted friend or colleague whose judgment you respect. And, use the "Crowd-Out-the-Crowd" form on the next page.

Exercise: *Crowd-Out-the-Crowd*

1. Think of some situation in which you can increase your personal power by making others aware of your competency. It might be a job-seeking situation. Or it could be a situation that puts you in control of resources. Or one that could be described as a "golden opportunity."

_____

_____

_____

_____

_____

_____

_____

2. Who must you impress to get the opportunity you described in #1?

_____

_____

_____

_____

3. What can you do to stand out from the crowd of people who are seeking to do the same thing?

_____

_____

_____

_____

_____

_____

4. Consider the approaches listed in the chart below. Then, in each of the next three columns write the word "possibly," "probably," or "definitely." As you answer, keep in mind the person you listed in question #2 and the action you described in question #3.

APPROACH	Will Understand	Will Appreciate	May Misinterpret
Doing something funny			
Doing something that is a departure from conventional practices			
Doing something that focuses attention on me			
Other(s):			

Review your responses. The approach that garners the most "definitelys" is the one you should explore further. Refine it. Get others' opinions. Then give it a try!

Paycheck

Why do people want more money? For most people, money allows freedom—the freedom to do what we choose to do without feeling guilty. Money also allows us to do good things for others. It represents a kind of power, too, in that it gives us the chance to refuse to do the things that do not appeal to us, refuse the places where we don't wish to be, refuse the work that does not interest us. Money, of course, can be viewed as a way to increase prestige as well, for the things it can buy often bespeak success.

There is nothing wrong with wanting more money—particularly in economically uncertain times. For those who wish to be prepared should a major illness strike or who are contemplating the reduced income of retirement, additional funds could translate to an important form of security.

Before reading this section on ways to increase your earning potential, briefly explain:

- Why you would like to earn more money.
- How much money you would like to have each year.
- What you would do with more.
- The people who would benefit from your increased income.
- How you could invest in yourself in order to earn more money.
- What additional schooling you might need.
- What your dream job is like and what it would pay.
- The skills/knowledge you already possess that could be a source of additional income.

_____

_____

_____

_____

_____

_____

_____

_____

_____

_____

_____

_____

_____

Study your responses. Are you willing to make the sacrifices that inevitably accompany the drive for increased wealth? What do you think those sacrifices will be?

To learn more about your paycheck-enhancing potential, answer "T" for true or "F" for false for each of the following statements.

T   F

☐ ☐ 1. I enjoy spending money.

☐ ☐ 2. I am not afraid of hard work.

☐ ☐ 3. I am considered ambitious.

☐ ☐ 4. I know what material possessions would make me happy.

☐ ☐ 5. I view money as a means of making my life and the lives of others more comfortable.

☐ ☐ 6. I believe in the saying, "If you always do what you've always done, you'll always get what you always got."

☐ ☐ 7. I am self-confident.

☐ ☐ 8. I believe I am not tapping my full potential.

☐ ☐ 9. I have established financial goals for myself.

☐ ☐ 10. I view wealth as one definition of success.

If you answered "true" to the majority of these questions, you probably have what it takes to dedicate yourself to making more money. You are probably aware of the downside to becoming wealthy, but you are probably also willing to work hard to enjoy the upside.

In the biographies of wealthy men and women, you will almost always find a devotion—not to money itself—but to the challenge of acquiring it.

"Ambitious" is the word we usually think of when we consider the men and women who have "made it big." People who are successful will always have critics, but if you intend to become such a person, you will have to put criticism and self-doubt in their rightful places. You will have to think of yourself in "ambitious" terms.

PROMOTION ACTIVITY #35:

Design a greeting card, one-liner, bumper-sticker slogan, or poster.

You can earn $5 to $500 per idea if you have the kind of creative bent necessary for designing greeting cards, bumper-sticker slogans, and posters. How do you go about breaking into this lucrative field? Go to a library and get the most current copy of the *Writer's Market,* published annually by Writer's Digest Books of Cincinnati, Ohio. Turn to the sections titled "Greeting Card Publishers" and "Humor" to learn who is paying what for which submissions. Names, addresses, telephone and fax numbers are provided, along with the guidelines for what publishers are seeking and what they will pay.

 PROMOTION ACTIVITY #36:

Become an entrepreneur.

In America, someone starts a home-based business every eleven seconds. We are indeed living in a time ripe with possibilities for entrepreneurs. One of the reasons for this entrepreneurial explosion is the fact that knowledge grows obsolete every six years (or less).

You do not have to quit your daytime job, nor do you have to invest a great deal of money in order to learn whether you have a product or service others would be willing to pay for. You need only to do some studying and be willing to invest some time to pilot your special idea. These are no longer womb-to-tomb employment times. Rather, today's worker needs to have several different irons in the professional fire in order to respond to changing corporate structures, changing technologies, and changing cultures.

Start now to learn about yourself, the market, and the entrepreneurial mind-set. There are all kinds of resources available to assist you. The chamber of commerce in nearly every major American city works with the Service Corps of Retired Executives (SCORE). These men and women donate their time and their wisdom to explain to businessowner-hopefuls what they will need to start businesses of their own. In addition, there is a plethora of books, magazines, and conferences on the very same topic. Beyond that, the Small Business Administration (SBA), local bank officers, and even small businessowners themselves are usually more than willing to share advice with people just starting out.

Begin thinking about what you enjoy doing and what you do well. Consider Kathy Lamb, an English teacher in Rochester, New York. In addition to being an outstanding educator, she is an outstanding pastry cook. Her specialty is pies, which her friends have always encouraged her to sell. She contacted several local restaurants and interested them in purchasing her "Lambie-pies." Similarly, Debbie Fields, with her special chocolate chip cookies, made the public aware of her sweet treats by giving away free samples in local malls. Encouraged by positive public responses, she subsequently built a chocolate empire.

Although you should not undertake any entrepreneurial project without first obtaining business, financial, and legal advice, you will follow a basic three-step pattern as you explore your entrepreneurial potential:

1. Determine what you have to sell.

2. Find out whether the public is willing to buy.

3. Set up your business on a limited scale and then expand as sales warrant.

The worksheet on the next page will help you determine whether you indeed have the entrepreneurial spirit. So, too, will the classic by Paul and Sarah Edwards, *The Best Home Businesses for the 90s*.

Exercise: Are You an Entrepreneur at Heart?

Answer "True," "False," or "Not Sure" to the following statements by placing a check mark in the appropriate column.

	True	False	Not Sure
1. I am willing to work hard.	☐	☐	☐
2. I would define myself as a risk-taker.	☐	☐	☐
3. I have a vision, a sense of the "big picture."	☐	☐	☐
4. I regard myself as a competitor.	☐	☐	☐
5. I often have original ideas.	☐	☐	☐
6. I believe this statement: Out of 2,000,000 millionaires, 90 percent own their own business.	☐	☐	☐
7. I can make decisions quickly.	☐	☐	☐
8. I have dreams of getting rich through my own efforts.	☐	☐	☐
9. I am highly motivated.	☐	☐	☐
10. When it comes to work, I would describe myself as a disciplined person.	☐	☐	☐

Analysis: Give yourself 10 points for each "true" response. Clearly, the more "trues" you have, the more certain are your entrepreneurial ambitions. A score of 70+ would indicate you have potential for starting your own business.

A simple psychological test may reveal an entrepreneurial drive. Somewhere in the space below, draw a circle that represents your past. Next—anywhere in the space below—draw a circle that represents your present life. Then—anywhere in the following space—draw a circle that represents your future.

Now examine the three circles carefully. Your first reaction may be one of bewilderment. You may wonder how psychologists could possibly look at circles and interpret meaning. And yet, assessments like the Rorschach test and other thematic apperception tests have been used successfully for years. Here are a few clues that may indicate insights into your motivational drives. Was your future circle the biggest of the three? That may indicate that you have confidence in your ability to fashion a successful future for yourself. Are your circles entwined. That, too, could have a positive connotation: you are interconnecting present, past, and future skills to achieve a beneficial outcome. If your past circle was the biggest of the three, it could suggest you are overly dependent on past successes. Discuss your drawing with a close friend. Ask each other questions about the possible meaning of what you have drawn. The validity of your mutual speculations is not as important as the probing you will do to learn what entrepreneurial risks, if any, you are willing to take.

PROMOTION ACTIVITY #37:

Invest.

No matter who you are, you can invest more than you do. Many of the things you have purchased are not must-have items, except perhaps in the emotional sense. Further, you can do many of the things you do in less expensive ways. To illustrate, many employees go to lunch each day. Assuming the average lunch is $5.00, you could save $100 a month just by bringing your lunch for a single month. If you smoke, giving up cigarettes will save you hundreds of dollars a year and will improve your health in the process.

Before you invest these newfound dollars, though, you must determine how much you *can* invest. You can make that decision by carefully analyzing your existing budget. Find out how much is going for what and then determine—through careful budgeting—how much more you could conceivably invest in a year.

The next logical step is to find a financial adviser—the yellow pages are filled with them. But before you contact a financial advisor, realize that directly or indirectly, there will be a charge for services. You may be perfectly willing to pay that fee, but first learn all you can free of charge by speaking to account representatives at your local bank. They can explain a great deal about long-term investments such as bonds, annuities, and other portfolio possibilities.

Once you have a general sense of the investment opportunities that are out there, you can begin your financial plan—with or without the help of professional planners. It will be important for you to prepare a net worth statement, which itemizes your assets and your liabilities. Next comes your budget or cash flow analysis, which compares your income to your expenses. The third item to consider is your intentions or plans for the future: Do you hope to own your own home in five years? Do you plan to take that $6,000 cruise you've been dreaming about? Do you have children who will be ready for college in nine years?

If you are beginning to think about retirement and its corollary, estate planning (actually, it's never too soon to begin), then you will, of course, need expert advice.

A certified financial planner can be counted on to give you no-nonsense information about tax planning, investments, and other items related to your net worth. Keep your ears open—in no time, you should hear about some relative, friend, or colleague who is using the services of a financial planner and who is pleased with those services. Very often, adult education programs offer sound financial advice for individuals seeking a financial checkup. They cover the basics, such as whether you have enough insurance (including disability insurance) and enough retirement income and whether you are budgeting as you should.

Your initial investment of time (and money, if you are hiring an expert) can pay off handsomely in the future. The sooner you start, the sooner you can expect to reap your rewards.

 PROMOTION ACTIVITY #38:

Get a part-time job.

You may wish to consider this possibility for just a short period of time—for example, in the fall to help you earn extra money for the holiday season. Or, you may be able to handle a year-round position if the sacrifice does not interfere severely with your health or your family responsibilities.

Where to begin? Check the want ads. See what looks possible, given your schedule, your needs, your interests. A second possibility is to work with an employment agency. Make them aware of what you are seeking and let them do the looking for you. Of course, they will charge you (in the form of lower wages) for the looking they do.

The advantage of part-time or seasonal work is that there is virtually no penalty for ending it. You don't have to worry that your career opportunities will be negatively impacted, especially if you make it clear in the beginning that you are accepting the position merely as a short-term assignment. When the stress becomes excessive or when you have earned all you need, you can simply terminate the assignment and be grateful for what you learned and earned while you had it.

PROMOTION ACTIVITY #39:

Ask to be compensated for a special project.

If your boss "farms out" some work to outside experts, you may be able to take advantage of this situation to earn extra money. To illustrate: The secretary to a Hollywood movie producer was aware of expenditures being made to "readers," people who read and critique movie scripts submitted to studios and independent producers.

In a move that was a bit risky, but which nonetheless caused her boss to look at her in a new light, she explained that she could use the extra money and asked if she could serve as a reader. Her boss was willing to give it a try and found that he was as pleased with her insights as he had been with the professional reader's comments.

Are there some things your organization is paying outsiders for—to make table decorations or to buy executive gifts or to plan parties? Is it possible for you to take on these extra duties without letting them interfere with your primary job?

Are you the sort of person who is willing to take the risk of asking? If so, you may find that more than financial advantages accrue.

# PROMOTION ACTIVITY #40:

Plan an event.

Three recently unemployed entrepreneurs decided to go into business together. Their "business" could be described by the vague and somewhat unusual term "event planners." Although they had absolutely no experience in planning events, they decided it could not be that difficult.

Their first call was to the managing director of a large professional association. They offered to plan the upcoming conference. To their complete surprise, the event planner agreed. Admittedly, they had a lot to learn and they made some mistakes along the way. But the event was more successful—at least in terms of enrollment—than the previous year's had been. To be sure, their learning curve will be shorter for the next event they plan.

Is this an income-increasing possibility for you? Would you be interested in handling the myriad of details associated with such work? Whom would you like to have on your team? What events could you plan? Parties, showers, conferences, charity events, weddings, and retirements are but a few. What experience do you have? What experience could you acquire before you attach the descriptor "event planner" to your business card?

This kind of work is not for everyone, but if you think you'd enjoy it, you could plan as many or as few events as your regular job permits. If you are successful at handling people, time, and details, you could probably develop this sideline into a very lucrative source of additional income. Don't do anything, though, until you speak—at great length—with people who *do* event planning. Call some local corporations and ask for the president's secretary, for example. Explain that you would like to learn more about event planning and ask whether you could be put in touch with the person at the firm who does that sort of thing.

Once you connect with the official or unofficial event planner, offer to take that person to lunch so that you don't impose on his or her work time. Then learn as much as you possibly can about this promising new means of fattening your paycheck.

PROMOTION ACTIVITY #41:

Ask to work overtime.

Discretionary time is considered the status symbol of the '90s. Many employees would rather threaten to strike than to be asked to work excessive overtime hours. And yet, if you are seeking to increase the size of your paycheck, overtime work represents a golden opportunity—especially if your family demands are limited.

Keep in mind that while your financial health may improve from overtime, your physical health may decline. And so, you may wish to set a limit—even if your employer does not—on the number of hours or months you are willing to devote to additional work. Too, if you find that your primary job begins to suffer because you are fatigued or stressed or rushed to the point of making mistakes, then you may opt to cut back the number of hours you have asked for.

Nonetheless, this temporary solution to the perpetual question "How can I earn more money?" may be the solution you are seeking.

 PROMOTION ACTIVITY #42:

Invest in yourself—the long-term benefit usually means higher income.

Pursuing an advanced degree is not easy—at any age. But it is particularly difficult for those who decide to earn it once they have begun working full time. By then, families grow and mortgages begin—and careers are in full swing. And yet, the number of "mature" students is growing as more and more employees realize the advantage of completing a degree program.

Speak with your boss, your mentor, and others you admire in the organization to learn which program is right for you, given your interests and long-range goals. Call the personnel department to find out whether the company will reimburse part or all of your tuition costs. If you do not work in an organization that does, you may have to consider loans or scholarship programs such as those offered by the American Business Women's Association (ABWA).

No one will deny the difficulty you face in earning your degree on a part-time basis. But the long-term result of such sacrifice is the potential for earning greater income. Are you ready to make that sacrifice? The Obstacle Courses exercise on the next page will help you find out.

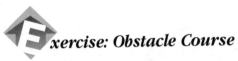 **xercise: Obstacle Course**

As you come to each obstacle on the path that leads from where you are now to the advanced education you hope to obtain, list at least three obstacles you will face at each of the points indicated by a barrier. (The first one, Personal Barriers, was done for you as an example.) Also list, on a scale of 1 (low) to 5 (high), the degree of confidence you have for overcoming those barriers.

DEGREE

Academic Barriers: _____

_____

_____

Confidence rating _____

Job or Professional Barriers: _____

_____

_____

Confidence rating _____

Family Barriers: _____

_____

_____

Confidence rating _____

Personal Barriers: _____

Do I have enough energy, time, money, determination, scholastic background?

_____

_____

Confidence rating _____

PRESENT CIRCUMSTANCES

# PROMOTION ACTIVITY #43:

Work on a free-lance basis.

If you have a special talent or skill, you may be able to parlay that into additional monies for your personal coffers. If you know how to prepare taxes, you can have a very profitable spring each year. If you have earned a real estate license, you can pick and choose the times when you would like to earn a little extra money. If you know how to do calligraphy or desktop publishing, if you can sew or cut hair or take beautiful photographs, if you can do household repairs or gardening, if you have artistic talent or proofreading skills, you can lend your abilities to selective assignments—as few or as many as you wish.

Consider the electrician, for example, who every December 1 begins putting up lights in lots around town from which Christmas trees are sold. It is the only time all year that he works outside his regular job, but he earns enough to do all his Christmas shopping.

Unlike working at a part-time job, which will have specific hours and definite obligations, and unlike starting your own entrepreneurial enterprise, which will require constant nurturing if you want it to grow, free-lancing leaves you "free" to do what you wish, when you wish.

Each of us has a skill, probably many skills, that can be converted into income-producing endeavors. The trick is finding out how we can serve and then who is willing to pay for our services.

Use the space below to brainstorm ways you could use your current skills to earn a free-lance income.

_____

_____

_____

_____

_____

_____

_____

_____

_____

_____

_____

_____

_____

_____

_____

_____

_____

_____

Ask around who is paying for what (snow plowing, raking, pool maintenance, dog-walking, child-care, home repairs, chauffering, catering, et cetera).

PROMOTION ACTIVITY #44:

Write an article for a trade journal.

Again, turn to the most current edition of the *Writer's Market* as the definitive source of paying customers—not only for greeting cards, one-liners, bumper-sticker slogans, and posters but also for longer pieces such as articles in journals or trade magazines. Avoid undertaking a lengthy and involved project, such as writing the great American novel or a major investigative opus. Such endeavors will surely consume you and leave you with no time, energy, or desire for your full-time job.

Instead, try a shorter piece—an article related to your industry or field. Yes, it will take time but nowhere near as much as a full-length book. Here is an example: *California Business* magazine pays up to $2,500 for articles of 2,000 to 4,000 words. If there are roughly seventy-five words in a paragraph (count the number in this paragraph), then forty paragraphs would give you 3,000 words. As you can see, writing a magazine article is not a daunting task.

Or if your field is architecture, *Inland Architect* will pay up to $300 for an article of 750 to 3,000 words. No matter what field you are in, there are publications related to it. If those publications are to stay in business month after month, they need a continuous stream of articles. Not only can you earn extra money this way, you can also earn additional prestige among your colleagues once your article appears in print.

If you're not sure whether writing's something you should pursue, take the quiz on the next page. It doesn't assess your actual writing skills, but it will open your eyes about what the writing process involves, in terms of skills, energy, and materials.

Exercise: Writing Quiz

Place a check mark in front of the statements that are "true" about you.

1. _____ I have always done well in English classes.

2. _____ I enjoy writing.

3. _____ I have access to a computer.

4. _____ I like to read.

5. _____ I like to explore ideas.

6. _____ Others have complimented me on my writing skills.

7. _____ I have a good vocabulary.

8. _____ I have been published before.

9. _____ The rules of grammar are not a mystery to me.

10. _____ I write quickly.

11. _____ I enjoy experimenting with various ways to make a point (using metaphors, comparison/contrast, analogies).

12. _____ I can organize ideas well.

13. _____ Using transitions is natural for me.

14. _____ I vary my sentence length and paragraph length automatically.

15. _____ My sentences do not all begin the same way.

16. _____ I find it fairly easy to persuade others.

17. _____ I enjoy painting word pictures.

18. _____ I am aware of the various tones and nuances that words create.

19. _____ I understand why passive voice is less effective than active.

20. _____ I own a thesaurus and a dictionary.

Scoring: The more check marks you have, the greater your literary proclivity. If you have only a few check marks, you have some work to do; but that doesn't mean you'll never be able to publish an article. Remeber, too, that you can hire an editor or ask a friend who's a stickler for grammar to help you with your weak areas.

# PROMOTION ACTIVITY #45:

Ask for a raise.

Of all the activities employees dread, this is the one that arouses the most fear—especially when they make the request during a performance appraisal, a time when their work is being reviewed and their future, in a sense, is being determined. Instead, ask for a raise about six months *after* your annual performance appraisal. That way, you can point out the improvements and advances you have made since then.

Here are some things for you to consider before, during, and after your meeting:

1. If possible, contact an employment agency before your meeting with your boss. Learn about the possibilities for a person of your experience and capability. Once you have had a chance to honestly appraise what the outside world has to offer a person with your skills and abilities, you will have a sense of how firm a negotiating stance you should take. You will be in a stronger position once you know how marketable you really are.

2. Prepare a list of the specific reasons why you feel you deserve a raise at this time. (Use The Raise Review form that follows.)

3. Be ready to ask for "concessions" if your request for a raise is denied. In other words, if you can't have a raise, what else would compensate in some way—a new title, additional training, being able to attend high-level meetings, being put in charge of a special project, cutting back on the number of hours you work, being able to work more hours at home, and so forth.

4. Make certain you have established a time that is convenient for your boss—don't simply catch him or her "on the run." Speaking of timing, it would be wise to choose a time for this discussion when you are working on a project in which you are demonstrating your value and worth. Consider, too, the economic times: Is your organization undergoing growth at this time, or is it downsizing? If the latter circumstance is true, you probably are fortunate enough to have a job. Attempting to increase your salary when others have been laid off will probably not be viewed favorably.

5. Have your boss acknowledge your value to the organization, if possible.

6. Try to remain calm and unemotional during this session.

7. If you sense that your supervisor is uncomfortable making the decision, suggest that you meet later, after he or she has had a chance to think about your request. If you have not heard anything in a week or so, ask for another meeting so you can resolve the issue.

8. If your request is denied, ask for a specific reason. Also ask when you might expect a raise and what you will have to do to increase your likelihood of receiving one.

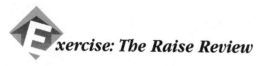

Exercise: The Raise Review

In the boxes on the left are "prompts," ideas to stimulate your thoughts about why you deserve a raise. In the box on the right, jot down what you would actually say about these factors. Once you have your presentation organized, rehearse it several times before you actually meet with your boss.

Reason for Deserving a Raise	What You Will Say
Your experience	
Your training and education	
Your loyalty and commitment	
Your people skills	
Your drive	
Your willingness to assist others	
Your personality	
The quality of your work	
Why you need more money	
How your salary compares to that of others doing comparable work	
How long it has been since your last raise	

PROMOTION ACTIVITY #46:

Begin bartering for services.

This recommendation is for saving money, not making it. Barter your services for services you need. Bartering is as old as America, but it is once again becoming so popular that dozens of bartering clubs have been formed across the nation. To be sure, you can engage in bartering practices in an informal way, or you can contact one of the bartering organizations and learn what can be exchanged for what.

Begin by thinking of something you need and approximately what it costs. Then think of what you could provide the firm or individual who could supply the needed item. What value would you place on the service? To illustrate, a grandmother in Albuquerque, New Mexico, living on a fixed income, makes holiday magnets and gives them to her dentist who—in return—gives her free teeth cleaning.

If you are interested in this unique way of obtaining what you need without expending your hard-earned money, read about what the town of Ithaca, New York, is doing. Then take the initiative and implement a bartering system of your own in your community.

> Tough times, it seems have been with us for years. Many of us have been hit pretty hard. That's why Paul Glover, a resident of Ithaca, New York, decided to do something about it. Two years ago he came up with a supplemental currency called HOURS, and here's how it works. Each HOUR is equivalent to one hour of time, or $10, which is the local county's average hourly wage. Also available are 1/4 HOURS ($2.50), 1/2 HOURS ($5) and 2 HOURS ($20), all printed from a small shop in town. You can buy all the goods and services you need just like you can with the U.S. dollar. You can even use HOURS to go to the movies or to enjoy some fine dining.
>
> Anyone can participate. For one dollar, residents become members and receive four HOURS automatically. *Ithaca Money,* the local newspaper established and published by Paul, lists all of the members, their phone numbers, and the services or goods they are either offering or seeking.*

* Reprinted with permission from *Mother Earth News,* August/September 1993, p. 33.

# PROMOTION ACTIVITY #47:

Consider joint payment for the things you need.

Just as time-sharing is a means of owning a condominium—for a slice of the calendar year—joint payment is a means of co-owning possessions. Think of a new ladder that you may need. You'd like the biggest and best model, but its cost is prohibitive, especially considering the fact that you probably use the ladder only a few times a year.

Joint payment allows you to pay half that amount and to have a friend or neighbor pay the other half. It is even possible to share ownership among several people. Of course, it is wise to form such arrangements with people you like and trust.

If you work in a small office in a large building, you may want to consider pooling equipment, or even support employees, with the other small offices on your floor. Everyone contributes to the cost, but everyone shares in the benefits as well.

Exercise: Joint Owership Options

1. What big-ticket items do you need? _____

_____

_____

2. How much does each one cost?

_____

_____

3. How many times a year do you need each one?

_____

_____

4. For those you do not need on a daily basis, would there be a storage problem if you kept the item for half the year and your co-payment partner kept it the other half?

_____

If there is a storage problem, do you live or work close enough to your partner to move the item back and forth between your homes or offices as needed?

_____

If neither of these options works, can you think of an equitable way to share the item? (If not, find another item that can be easily rotated between the locations.) _____

_____

5. Of the friends, neighbors, and business acquaintances you have, who would be the best partner to share the expense and rotation with? _____

_____

6. What services (gardening, cleaning, child care, etc.) could you share with a friend, colleage, or family member? _____

_____

_____

 PROMOTION ACTIVITY #48:

Hold training classes.

Think about holding a class for a small group of people in your home, church, basement, or local craft store. There are people who teach others how to make corn-husk dolls, how to do stenciling, how to decorate cakes. Do you have a teachable skill? To remind yourself of all you know how to do well, scan the offerings in a local community college catalog, an adult education catalog, or a catalog from places such as the nationwide Learning Annex.

A woman on the West Coast holds Saturday classes for up to twenty people in the basement of her home. The topic: how to break into the speaking business. The cost: $350 per person. Calculate the coins she gathers in a single day.

You can probably do something similar and do it very well. Begin to make inquiries. Contact your local newspaper about the cost (if any) of running an advertisement about your class.

Consider doing the first few classes free of charge—to build up your following and your reputation as well. There is a third advantage: each time you conduct the class, you will refine your technique and your materials.

PROMOTION ACTIVITY #49:

Offer suggestions for cash awards.

Ideally, your organization already has a cash-award program that offers monetary prizes for employees who suggest ideas that will save corporate time and money. (If there is no such program, by the way, consider taking the opportunity to develop one. There are thousands of precedents for you to cite, including organizations that currently use suggestion programs. Be prepared to point out the benefits for all concerned.

All processes can be improved. It will take some time, some data-gathering, some analysis, some proposal-preparation to convince senior management, but individually or as a team member—you can make operations better than they currently are. Many teams—in both private and public organizations—are rewarded for the savings they effect.

Your idea may not pertain to processes. It may not involve other people directly. But it should benefit you as well—if only as another item you can add to your list when you have your raise-request meeting.

If there is no hope that your firm will reward you financially or if you are self-employed or unemployed, you can still earn extra money. Read the newspaper carefully, looking for opportunities that offer money in exchange for bright ideas. A fluorocarbon company, several years ago, was seeking a new name. It turned to the public and offered a $5,000 prize to the person who submitted the best idea. Stay attuned to these possibilities—they may represent the opportunity you have been looking for.

An offshoot of this idea, of course, is to bring an invention or a new idea to the market. We all have good ideas for new products. Most of us, unfortunately, do not pursue our ideas. If you have an idea you want to pursue, first get honest reactions from friends and family members. (A caveat here: use good judgment as you gather feedback. If your idea really is a marketable one, you do not want to lose it to an unscrupulous person who obtains a patent on it before you do!)

If the response from those who try it is favorable, you need to contact a patent attorney to help you conduct a patent search. (It is possible to do this yourself, but it means reviewing all the patent applications that are similar. The product, after all, could already have a patent on it. The applications are in the Washington, D.C.,

Patent Office. It is, however, best that you seek professional assistance for this search.) If the patent does not exist, you can obtain one for the product by filling out the necessary forms provided by the U.S. Patent Office.

Once you own the patent, you have one final choice to make: Do you wish to begin manufacturing the product yourself or do you wish to sell the patent to a manufacturing firm?

This, of course, is simply a thumbnail sketch of the process. For the fullest details—even if you intend to hire an attorney to handle the details—books such as *Patent It Yourself! How To Protect, Patent, and Market Your Inventions* by David Pressman are a valuable resource.

PROMOTION ACTIVITY #50:

Get a higher-paying job.

This recommendation is presented last because—in this decade of job insecurity—leaving a secure position in search of a job that may pay a higher wage is not always a good idea. First of all, there are other factors to be considered—enjoyment of the work, positive relationships with your co-workers and boss, opportunities to learn and grow, a relaxed but professional atmosphere, fringe benefits, proximity to home, promotional possibilities. Never give up a job *simply* because you wish more money.

However, if you cannot think of a single compelling reason to remain, if you are a risk-taker, if more money is important to you, if you have savings you can live on for several months, and if you do not have a family dependent upon your steady income, then you may wish to *consider* searching for a higher-paying job.

As always, there are books available to assist you if you select this option. To name but a few:

The 100 Best Jobs for the 1990's and Beyond by Carol Kleiman

Where the Jobs Are by John W. Wright

What Color Is Your Parachute? by Richard Nelson Bolles

Money is not the answer to all problems, but it can certainly solve a few. If you select this option as a way to increase your income, good luck. Your vision can lead to victory, but be prepared to suffer a few of the slings and arrows that outrageous fortune shoots at each of us.

Biding Your Time

4

Promoting Yourself was written primarily as encouragement for those of you whose corporate promotion has not come as quickly or as easily as you had hoped. Throughout this book, you've been asked to consider the reasons behind your desire for a promotion. You've been offered dozens of alternatives for increasing your power, your prestige, and your pay—the typical reasons people list for wanting a promotion. Any one of these recommendations has more immediate potential for increasing your power, prestige, or pay than a promotion does.

However, if your dream is to enter the managerial ranks; if you persist in regarding a promotion as the best way to increase your power, prestige, or pay; if you have chosen to devote your energies to corporate promotion rather than to self-promotion, then here are a few suggestions:

- Set up a time to meet with your boss for a career-planning session. Frankly but diplomatically, you will essentially say, "Here is where I am. Over here is where I want to be in three years. What do I need to do to get there?"

  Following this discussion, find out whether your boss is willing to help you get there. If the answer is "no," you will want to know that now so that you don't labor under the false assumption that your boss is helping to advance your career. Knowing early also allows you time to find someone else to guide you. If the answer is "yes," then you know you can count on this person to advise you, to help you make the right decisions, the right moves. No matter what the answer, though, thank your boss for the time he or she has taken to explore your career path with you.

- If your boss declined to serve as your mentor, find someone else, inside or outside the organization, with whom you can share your ambitions and your strategies for achieving them. Ideally, the person you select will have experience and wisdom as well as creative and listening skills. Although that person need not be in the same field as yours, he or she should be someone whose success and ethics you trust.

- Make yourself known. You need not pursue attention in a self-aggrandizing fashion, but you should make others aware of what you have done and of what you can do. "Power does not flow to invisible people," the old saying goes. A newer saying is relevant as well, this one from Dr. Adele Scheele, "It's a myth that in the business world if you're good you'll be discovered." You must help others discover you and what you can do for the organization. Even if you are not paid extra now, creating an additional job title for yourself (with your boss's approval) could yield lucrative benefits in the future. To illustrate, if you are a secretary and would like to serve in a managerial capacity for other secretaries, you might consider being the director of secretarial services. As such, you would distribute information of interest to the company's secretaries. Or plan a special way to honor them during National Secretaries Month in

April. Working with a team of volunteers, you might even plan a secretarial conference. Who knows? Your self-created job may one day lead to a paying job. (See Marilyn Lewis's story on page 18.)

- List the five people in the organization whose success you most admire. Write a memo asking for a twenty-minute "interview" with each of them over the next six months. Explain that you admire their success and that you hope one day to emulate it. Ask when it would be convenient to meet with them to learn more about the factors that contributed to that success. Take extensive notes at the interview (you may even want to tape record it). Afterwards, assimilate the information and convert it to a plan of action.

- Begin a file of information about successful individuals. The articles can be from magazines or newspapers. Or, you can make notes on books you have read by and about successful business people. Let them serve as your inspiration. Keep motivational quotations in there as well. Before you go to work each morning, take five minutes to review one thing from your file. Let it serve as your inner voice throughout the working day.

- Reach outside the company, even outside the country. Do what Fernanda M.M.N. Colasso of Sao Paulo, Brazil, did. After hearing at a seminar about a successful team at Mount Carmel Medical Center in Columbus, Ohio, Fernanda decided to serve as an international liaison. She is now serving as the benchmarking connection: sharing information she receives from the medical center with her colleagues in Brazil. All it took was a few minutes to establish the international connection.

There is no guarantee that these suggestions will lead to a promotion. But life does not offer guarantees. The best you can do is promote yourself and be guaranteed that you have done something to achieve greater power and prestige, or a bigger paycheck in one way or another. By taking action, you can be guaranteed that you fall into the category of people who make things happen instead of letting them happen. If your organization does not promote you, you can certainly promote yourself and the causes you believe in.

Bibliography

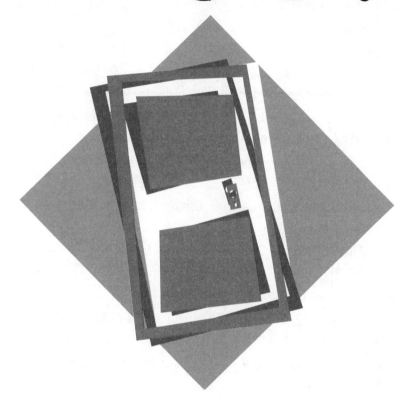

and Suggested
Reading

Bardwick, Judith. *The Plateau Trap: How to Avoid It in Your Career—and Your Life*. New York: American Management Association, 1986.

Bolles, Richard Nelson. *What Color Is Your Parachute?* Berkeley, CA: Ten Speed Press, 1994.

Buskirk, Richard H. *Your Career: How to Plan It, Manage It, Change It*. Boston: CBI Publishing, 1980.

Caroselli, Marlene. *Meetings That Work*. Mission, KS: SkillPath Publications, 1991.

Caroselli, Marlene and David Harris. *Risk-Taking: 50 Ways to Turn Risks Into Rewards*. Mission, KS: SkillPath, Publications, 1993.

Clarke, Colleen. *Networking: How to Creatively Tap Your People Resources*. Mission, KS: SkillPath Publications, 1993.

Csikszentmihalyi, Mihaly. *Flow: The Psychology of Optimal Experience*. New York: Harper & Row, 1990.

Edwards, Paul and Sarah Edwards. *The Best Home Businesses for the 90s*. New York: Putnam, 1991

Feder, Michal E. *Taking Charge: A Personal Guide to Managing Projects and Priorities*. Mission, KS: SkillPath Publications, 1989.

Fulghum, Robert. *Uh-Oh*. New York: Villard Books, 1991.

Funkhouser, G. Ray. *The Power of Persuasion: A Guide to Moving Ahead in Business and Life*. New York: Random House, 1986.

Friedman, Paul. *How to Deal With Difficult People*. Mission, KS: SkillPath Publication, 1991.

Girard, Joe. *How to Sell Yourself*. New York: Warner Books, 1992.

Givens, Charles J. *SuperSelf: Doubling Your Personal Effectiveness*. New York: Simon & Schuster, 1993.

Good, Sharon. *Managing With a Heart*. New York: Excalibur Publishing, 1994.

Hyatt, Carole and Linda Gottlieb. *When Smart People Fail: Rebuilding Yourself for Success*. New York: Penguin Books, 1993.

Jackson, Tom. *Guerrilla Tactics in the New Job Market*. New York: Bantam Books, 1991.

Kleiman, Carol. *The 100 Best Jobs for the 1990's and Beyond*. Berkley Publishing Group, 1994.

Lewis, Adele and Doris Kuller. *Fast-Track Careers for the 90s*. Glenview, IL: Scott, Foresman Company, 1990.

Mackay, Harvey. Sharkproof: *Get the Job You Want, Keep the Job You Love—In Today's Frenzied Job Market*. New York: HarperBusiness, 1993.

Poley, Michelle Fairfield. *A Winning Attitude: How to Develop Your Most Important Asset!* Mission, KS: SkillPath Publications, 1992.

Posner, Mitchell J. *Executive Essentials: The Comprehensive Guide to What Every Business Person Ought to Know to Stay Ahead*. New York: Avon Books, 1982.

Pressman, David. *Patent It Yourself! How to Protect, Patent, and Market Your Inventions*. New York: McGraw-Hill, 1979.

Shouse, Deborah. *Breaking the Ice: How to Improve Your On-The-Spot Communication Skills*. Mission, KS: SkillPath Publications, 1994.

Stone, W. Clement. *The Success System That Never Fails*. New York: Simon & Schuster, 1980.

Temme, Jim. *Productivity Power: 250 Great Ideas for Being More Productive*. Mission, KS: SkillPath Publications, 1993.

Towers, Mark. *The ABC's of Empowered Teams: Building Blocks for Success*. Mission, KS: SkillPath Publications, 1994.

Wright, John W. *Where the Jobs Are*. New York: Avon Books, 1992.